Proposal
Best
Practices

Proposal Best Practices

A Practical Guide to Improve Your Win Rate When Responding to RFPs

David Seibert

PROPOSAL BEST PRACTICES

Seibert, David.   Proposal Best Practices : a practical guide to improve your win rate when responding to RFPs

ISBN-13: 978-0-578-54454-0

Cincinnati, Ohio, United States

Dedicated to Donna, my wonderful wife,
and my three awesome children,
Lyndsay, Kelly, and Ben.

Table of Contents

Acknowledgements

I've always thought the acknowledgements section at the front of books was a waste of paper. These sections are typically corny, overwhelmingly sappy, and generally never worth reading unless you are one of the people being written about.

Then I wrote a book and I thought, "Gee! What a great idea!"

First and foremost, I must acknowledge and thank Dr. Tom Sant, author of *Persuasive Business Proposals* among many others, founder of The Sant Corporation (later Qvidian and now Upland Qvidian), APMP Fellow, a thought leader in the proposal field, a humorist, and an all-around nice guy. When I first met Tom, I had already embraced a consultative approach to selling—except where it involved proposals. Tom straightened me out. I remember one day he handed me a binder. It must have been three inches thick and it was packed cover to cover with enough pages to ensure it would never be read.

"Who's going to read that?" I laughed.

"Look at the binding," he responded. As I heaved the massive binder sideways and read the words, Volume I, Tom dropped Volume II onto the table. The sound of Volume II's weighty mass on the wooden table reverberated around the small conference room with a mighty THUD that startled me and, no doubt, the people on the floor below.

"Exactly," he responded with a grin. Lesson learned.

Over the last two decades, I've learned much about writing proposals from attending the School of Hard Knocks—just rolling up my sleeves and doing it, making mistakes, learning from them, making more mistakes, and learning from them, too. Still, it was Tom that got me started down the path. I am his student and I am building on his work. Thank you, Tom.

I never anticipated how much work is involved in drafting, reviewing, and editing, and then re-drafting, re-reviewing, and re-editing a book. It's a lot. And it wouldn't have been possible without the extraordinary and insightful efforts of my friend, Dr. David Nealey, President of WordSmart Business Services, bid forensics consultant, and application developer. Despite his busy schedule, David still found time to review early manuscripts and provide excellent feedback and advice. This book is far better because of his involvement. Thank you, David.

Thanks to my sister, Sheila, for reviewing the manuscript and giving much needed advice from the perspective of a procurement person. Her feedback was insightful, and her enthusiastic support came at a much needed moment. Thank you, Sheila.

Finally, I'd be remiss if I didn't also thank my dad, Tom Seibert, for teaching me so much about so many things. I am my father's son. A college professor he was, and a college professor I should have been. I took a different path, but not as far off the path as it might seem. In my efforts to teach the business world about selling and proposals—through so many training classes, webinars, consulting engagements, and now in this book—I think I did, ultimately, follow in his giant footsteps. I will never be able to claim that I've been such a powerful influence in the positive formation of so many young adults, but if I'm able to improve the lives of just a fraction of the people he influenced over his long and distinguished career, over his long life, I am a very happy man. Thanks, Dad.

Preface

Writing a proposal in response to an RFP is not a writing project to complete, it's a selling opportunity to win. This is the fundamental premise on which this entire book is built, so this is where we begin.

Far too many businesses treat RFPs as if they are writing projects to complete, questionnaires to finish, projects to check off someone's to do list. When an RFP comes in the door, their focus is to complete it—*as quickly and efficiently as possible*. They approach the entire effort almost as if it's a numbers game; the more RFPs they respond to, the more they're going to win. They're wrong.

HOW TO IMPROVE YOUR WIN RATE

If you want to make a good pot roast, you can't just throw a chuck roast and some carrots in a pan and expect good results. A good pot roast has a list of ingredients, and you have to include them all—in the right order and with the right preparation—if you expect good results. Pursuing RFP opportunities is no different.

If you want to improve your win rate—*if you want to win more of the RFP opportunities you pursue*—you cannot limit your business development effort to just one ingredient, you must do them all:
- **Selling**. Implement an effective pre-RFP selling program.
- **Configuring solutions**. Customize awesome solutions unique to each buyer.
- **Messaging**. Create messaging targeted to the buyer's needs.
- **Writing**. Write proposals that are persuasive, compelling, customer-focused, and that differentiate your solution.

Do these things well and you will win more opportunities more consistently. Don't do these things and you won't. It's really that simple.

WHY I WROTE THIS BOOK

Over the years, I've worked with many businesses that were motivated to improve their win rates but they didn't know how to do it. That's why I wrote this book; to explain how to do it. *Proposal Best Practices* documents the most important business practices that every business should implement if they're serious about improving their win rate when pursuing opportunities and responding to RFPs.

WHO THIS BOOK IS FOR

This book is not just about writing proposals, it's about improving your win rate. Therefore, this book is not only for proposal writers, it's for everyone involved in the business development effort. This includes salespeople, sales and marketing support staff, subject matter experts, small business owners, and everyone else who is involved in or contributes to the effort.

REAL LIFE LESSONS FOR REAL LIFE PROBLEMS

The information in this book is a culmination of the most important concepts and ideas and tricks and lessons that I've collected or developed over the years—all of which I learned while managing difficult sales territories with unrealistic quotas, and responding to disorganized RFPs mandating unreasonable requirements with unrealistic deadlines. In other words, real life stuff.

I hope you enjoy it, and I hope you profit from it.

-Dave Seibert

Executive Introduction

1. What Are Best Practices, Who Decides, and How Do You Implement Them?

'Best practice' is a widely used term in today's business world. Whenever I hear it, though, I always ask myself, *best practice according to whom*? It's a good question to ask because there is no such thing as universal agreement on what the term actually means. Indeed, best practice has become something of a buzzword in much of the business world. It's a term that many people employ and banter about with little regard for its technical accuracy.

Here are three instances in which it's fair and appropriate to ask, *"best practice according to whom?"*

1. Disagreement over what best practices should be

When I was doing research for this book, I searched the Internet using the term, "best practices for writing proposals." Of the many sites listed, I was surprised to find one advocating sellers should begin their proposals with a well-written overview of their company. I was surprised because to my way of thinking—and to most other proposal professionals I know—this qualifies as a *worst* practice, not a best practice. You *never, ever* want to begin a proposal talking about yourself. It's always much better to begin a proposal by talking about the buyer, acknowledge what they want to accomplish, and then explain how you are going to help them get what they want.

Whether you agree with me and the majority of proposal professionals or this other person, it's important to recognize there are different people in the industry advocating contrarian approaches to the same issue, and both maintaining their approach is a best practice. You have to evaluate the person advocating the practice and decide, for yourself, whether he or she is credible. This is reason number one why you ask, *"best practice according to whom?"*

2. Best practices are not all universally applicable across an industry

Industries large enough to have a professional association usually empanel a group or standards committee responsible for identifying, researching, and adopting industry best practices. By formalizing best practices in this way, the association creates an industry-wide standard that all of its professionals can reference and aspire to. Despite this, universal standards often do not work well for every organization that operates in an industry.

In the proposal world, for example, large federal contractors typically use sophisticated pursuit and capture processes. In this environment, it's a best practice to have multiple color-coded review teams and decision gates at various points throughout the process.

While these practices are great for large federal contractors, they're generally far too involved for small businesses that lack the infrastructure and staff of their larger counterparts. Smaller vendors just don't have the people or budgets to do anything more than the basics.

Therefore, if a standards association says it's a best practice to have a formalized review process, that's OK. However, if they say the review must include a sophisticated, multistep process involving multiple review teams and multiple decision steps, then it's no longer a best practice. It can't be since it can't reasonably be implemented by many or even the majority of practitioners in the market.

This is reason number two why you have to ask, *"best practice according to whom?"* Or maybe in this case, *"best practices for whom?"*

3. An industry is too small to have generally accepted best practices

While working for one of my clients, I encountered an RFP question asking how 'we implement industry best practices.' I chuckled when I read the question. The market into which my client is selling is small—a niche market if there ever was one. What I found most interesting, though, is that among the two serious competitors in this small market, their views on best practices vary significantly, but the variances are based largely on their internal capabilities. For example, if they have a capability they think is unique, they tout it as a best practice. If they fall short of a competitor's capability, however, they dismiss it as unnecessary. In other words, 'best practice' in this scenario is not really about which practices are best. Instead, the 'best practices' moniker is distorted and twisted into a marketing device that is not necessarily tied to actual best practices; if it looks good in a proposal and we can actually do it, then we'll call it a best practice. If not, we'll dismiss it as unnecessary or misguided.

This is reason number three why you have to ask, "best practice according to whom?"

These three examples demonstrate the challenge when using a term like *best practice*—there is no universal agreement or rule or regulation on what it means or how it should be implemented. Depending on who you are speaking with, a best practice could be a technical specification that is formal and codified (such as a formal ISO specification), it could be more like a guideline, or it could be little more than someone's biased opinion.

This is precisely why, as we begin our discussion of best practices, it's necessary to ask and then answer, *"what is a best practice?"*

WHAT IS A BEST PRACTICE?

For our purposes in this book, a best practice has two fundamental components.

1. It must be widely used among proposal and business development professionals and generally agreed to consistently produce good results.

2. It must be feasible for all businesses in the field to implement as stated, or it must be sufficiently general that all businesses have the flexibility to customize it to work in their business.

Widely used and generally agreed

I readily admit the first part of this definition has lots of wiggle room, especially the part that reads, "widely used...generally agreed...to consistently produce good results." It goes to the heart of why I felt the need to write this chapter—*according to whom?*

Recognizing this, each chapter in this book includes not just the best practice, but also the rationale behind why I call it a best practice. This way, you can evaluate for yourself whether you agree it actually is a best practice.

Feasible to implement

Adopting a best practice into your sales and proposal operation is much like buying a new suit. Suppose I say, "it is a best practice to wear a suit to a wedding." Notice I don't say what kind of suit, what color, or whether you should wear a bow tie or a neck tie. All I say is 'you should wear a suit.' It's up to you to decide how to implement that best practice, or in this case, decide what kind of suit to buy.

Personally, I like a traditional cut, three button, navy blue suit with a white shirt and a red tie. Maybe you prefer one of those new-fangled suits that look two sizes too small and are far too tight around the middle. I don't, but what I think doesn't matter. The only thing that matters is you take that best practice—*you should wear a suit to a wedding*—then understand it, consider it in all its implications, and make it your own.

Choosing how to implement proposal best practices is no different than choosing which suit to buy. For example, it is a best practice to have a proofreading process in place before you submit a proposal to a buyer. Even though this practice is applicable to everyone, you have ultimate discretion in how you actually implement the practice. A large federal contractor that operates a large proposal development organization will likely employ on-staff proofreaders who evaluate proposal documents against a corporate style manual. A small seller, in contrast, may implement a modest review process built around Molly at the front desk—because everyone knows she remembers all of the grammar rules she was taught in school and she finds every mistake every time.

It doesn't matter how you implement your review process. It only matters that you spend time considering it, implement it in a way that is appropriate for your company and, once implemented, it's effective.

ADVICE FOR IMPLEMENTING BEST PRACTICES

When I'm teaching a proposal class and I share the best practices sellers should be using, most of the people in the class recognize why these things are best practices. They can even envision the benefits that will come from implementing them. Despite this, most organizations don't always do well implementing what they've learned.

This should come as no surprise, though. People understand that smoking is bad for them but many are still unable to quit. Most of us understand the importance of exercise but still fail to do it regularly. Change can be difficult.

Organizational change is difficult

Like individual change, organizational change is also difficult. We're starting with a group of people used to doing something one way, and we're asking them to do that same thing differently.

Most resist. Some resist because they don't understand or appreciate the reason for the change. Others resist because they don't know how to make the change. Still others resist because they don't have the resources to implement the change. And of course, there are always those who resist because they're lazy.

Whatever the reason, when time is short and deadlines are looming, they quickly fall back on old habits: "This is the way we've always done it!"

The bottom line is it's not enough to take a training class or read a book to learn something new, changing behavior requires more. There must be mechanisms in place to ensure best practices are actually implemented, and even more, that they're embraced.

Helping your organization embrace change

There are five specific things you can do to increase the likelihood your staff will adopt proposal best practices and incorporate them into their day-to-day efforts.

1. Find a manager to sponsor the change

You can't change staff behavior unless there is a manager within the organization—someone with authority—who believes the change is important and necessary, and who's willing to invest the time to ensure it actually happens.

Good or bad, right or wrong, you can't just tell people to change their behavior and then reasonably expect they will. So in addition to telling them how you want them to change, you have to demonstrate the same change yourself, you have to expect it in others, and you have to follow up so everyone knows you're serious. And then, over time, people will get it, they'll adopt it, and it will become the new norm.

When you want to change organizational behavior you must be clear, you must be persuasive, and you must also be persistent.

2. Explain why the change is important

It's far easier for people to adopt a new practice if they understand why it's necessary. To the point, they must understand the problem that is prompting the change, and how the new process or practice solves the problem. If they understand the reasoning behind the change, they'll be less likely to resist and more likely to help facilitate the change you are proposing.

3. Provide training to your staff

This is a big one.

It is unrealistic to tell someone to change and then expect them to have the knowledge or ability to faithfully implement the change you expect. You can proclaim, for example, "all proposal writers should write persuasively." This certainly seems to make sense, but for people who have never been educated in persuasive writing skills, even if they are willing to make the change, they don't know how to do it.

In addition to communicating the change you want, therefore, you must also provide your staff with resources or training so they know *how* to do what you expect.

4. Involve staff in planning its implementation

It stands to reason people are more engaged in a new process or program if they feel they have a say in its formation, if they feel invested in its success.

> *This is not just a new process being forced on me, it's a process I helped create. This is my process!*

If your employees take this kind of ownership, they're more likely to manage it better over time. For example, if two months into the new program, a part of the program is not working as well as it should, your staff is more likely to propose changes to make it work better. This is precisely the kind of employee engagement managers dream about.

There always needs to be someone who drives the planning of the new program—a manager who keeps it on track and ensures everyone is working within a framework. But including everyone else in the effort to "build out" the framework will go a long way toward ensuring the new process and framework is adopted and implemented.

5. Hold staff accountable

Ultimately, successful change requires every person involved in the transition be held accountable for his or her role in implementing the change. This is especially difficult in the proposal world because we're always dealing with deadlines. When there's still a lot of work to be done but not a lot of time left to complete it, many proposal writers will do what they always do; they plug in content from previous proposals. When this happens, the change you're trying to make, the best practices you're trying to implement, take a back seat to the urgency of the moment.

These people are not necessarily antagonists and contrarians whose aim is to undermine your effort to change. Most of the time, they're regular people overwhelmed with too much work.

Despite that, unless and until you hold your staff accountable for making the changes you're trying to implement, even during these high-pressure moments, nothing will ever change.

Change is not easy, and it does not happen overnight. But these five measures, along with equal parts of patience and persistence, will eventually produce the change—and the results—you want.

CHAPTER RECAP

A best practice is a practice that is widely used among proposal professionals and generally agreed to produce better or best results. It's something you should implement within your proposal and business development organizations.

Despite this, a best practice is a guideline, something to aspire to. In this book, at least, it's not defined so much as described. You are the one who gets to decide how to implement it within your organization and make it your own.

Implementing organizational change is difficult. It requires persuasion, lots of patience, and persistence. But there are five things you can do to improve your chances.

1. Find a manager to sponsor the change
2. Explain why the change is important
3. Provide training to your staff
4. Involve staff in planning the implementation of the change
5. Hold staff accountable

2. The Most Important Best Practice: Be Proactive

Can you step in during the last 100 yards of a 26-mile marathon and have a realistic hope of winning the race? Of course not. You'd be disqualified. The winner is going to be the person who's run the most effective marathon and then follows it up with a strong sprint at the end.

The same goes for RFPs and proposals. When your competitors are selling to buyers in the 24 months before an RFP is issued—meeting people and getting to know them, establishing credibility, solving problems, educating decision makers, influencing the influencers, etc.—what makes you think you can swoop in at the very end and win the deal? You can't do it in marathons, you can't do it in the world of professional selling, and you're arrogant if you think otherwise.

Reactive selling doesn't work

Many sellers are almost totally reactive. They believe if they receive an RFP—even if it's one they weren't expecting and know little or nothing about—it represents a sales opportunity they have a legitimate chance at winning. They're wrong.

Yes, you may win one of these RFP opportunities every once in a while—just like I'm able to hit a long, straight tee shot every once in a while. But I can't build a golf career on my tee shot any more than you can build a business on 'every once in a while.'

This should come as no surprise, though. After all, who would hire another company to provide an important product or service if all they had to base their decision on was some text written on a piece of paper? What responsible decision maker would hire a payroll company (or a relocation company, or a printing company, or an IT company, or a staffing company, or a communications company, or a fulfillment house, or a recruiting firm, etc., etc.) if the only thing they knew about that company was what's included on the pages of a proposal?

Responsible business people DO NOT make strategic purchase decisions that way. There's too much at risk to base their decisions solely on what's written on the pages of a proposal.

HOW PROCUREMENTS REALLY WORK

When faced with making a procurement decision, *responsible* decision makers usually invest time educating themselves about whatever it is they anticipate buying. They learn about the relevant vendors, meet with the experts in each of those companies, understand each vendors' organizational approaches to service and pricing and delivery and support, and in general, do all of the things that responsible decision makers do before making important buying decisions.

What's important to understand is this discovery and decision-making process doesn't happen *after* the buyer receives proposals back from vendors, it typically happens in the 12-24 months *before* the buyer issues an RFP.

What this means is sellers need to be engaging buyers at that critical point when buyers are doing their discovery and forming their opinions and making their decisions. If a seller waits until the RFP comes in the door and only then marshals resources to respond, they're too late. Too much work has already been done. Too many decisions have already been made. Too many decision makers have already decided on their favorite vendor or vendors—and if you haven't been engaged with the buyer before the RFP, you probably aren't one of them.

The following graph illustrates well what happens before and after an RFP is issued.

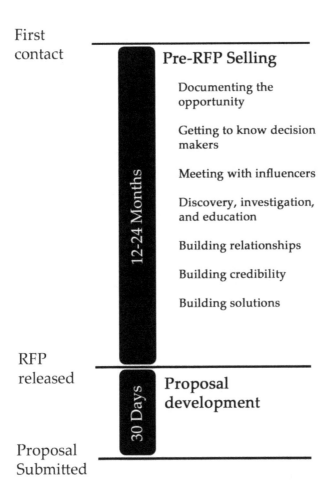

First contact

Pre-RFP Selling

Documenting the opportunity

Getting to know decision makers

Meeting with influencers

Discovery, investigation, and education

Building relationships

Building credibility

Building solutions

12-24 Months

RFP released

Proposal development

30 Days

Proposal Submitted

To put some perspective to this discussion, let's review a procurement from both the buyer's and the seller's perspectives.

A procurement from the buyer's perspective

Sally Jones is the VP of Accounting, and she's faced with choosing a payroll vendor for her firm. Her decision affects all of her employees, and it reflects directly on her, so she takes it seriously. The consequences are great enough she would never consider just sitting down one day to review a bunch of proposals without having invested any prior consideration.

Therefore, over the 24 months before she releases the next RFP, she's thinking about the decision she's facing. She already knows who the relevant vendors are, including which ones she likes and which ones she doesn't. She's already talked, at length, to their current vendor's senior manager, and they've discussed what the vendor would do differently if their contract was renewed. She's also met with the top two competitors to the current vendor. Last Saturday, when she met her friend for lunch, she asked what vendor her friend's company was using and what she thought of them.

Let's put this into perspective. It's still six months before the RFP is issued and she's already developed a pretty good understanding about the strengths and weaknesses of each vendor, who she likes and who she doesn't, who she's comfortable with and who makes her uncomfortable, who her staff likes and who they don't, etc. Sally is not going into this decision without some forethought or consideration; in fact, it's just the opposite. Sally has thought about it, she's considered it, she's developed all kinds of preconceptions, and she's come to many conclusions—and all of this has happened in the years *before* the RFP goes out.

Now the RFP goes out.

Sally has already figured out the two vendors she favors, but she didn't share this with Joe in the procurement department. Joe's job, after all, is to ensure a competitive bid process. Besides, the last thing Joe would ever do would be to limit the field to these two vendors—even though these are the only two companies Sally is seriously considering. So Joe sends the RFP to seven different vendors who all seem to fit the profile for the payroll services Sally and company require.

A procurement from a seller's perspective

Now let's look at the same procurement, but let's do it from a seller's perspective.

You're sitting at your desk wondering what you're going to do with your life for the next four weeks when, voila!, an RFP arrives at your door. Your company is not one of the two companies Sally is seriously considering, it's one of the seven Joe selected to receive the RFP. But you don't know that.

Even though you've never spoken to Sally before, even though you have no relationship with this buyer, you high five one of your colleagues and exclaim, "Woohoo! This is right up our alley."

So you pull together your team, write an awesome proposal, sweat over the details and the pricing, and then submit what you are sure is the winning bid.

And then you lose.

The harsh reality

This entire story is fictional, but it's not made up. The same story line plays out all the time, day after day, with thousands of companies across the world. It's fueled by procurement officers who want their procurements to be as competitive as possible, and unsuspecting sellers who are gullible enough to believe them, who actually think they have a chance at winning business from someone they don't know and have never met.

This description, though harsh, is an accurate representation of how the process really works; if you don't know someone before the RFP comes out, your chances of winning are small, really small, almost nil.

But, hey, don't lose hope. You may have lost this time, but that doesn't mean you have to spend the rest of your career responding to RFPs you are pre-ordained to lose. You can start winning...*but only if you want to*. It's totally up to you.

MOVING FROM REACTIVE TO PROACTIVE

If you want to start winning more RFPs, more consistently, stop being reactive. Instead of waiting for an RFP to fall in your lap, you need to proactively identify opportunities ahead of time, and then you need to go get them. You need to qualify those opportunities. You need to work through the investigation and discovery steps. You have to go meet people, build relationships, and identify each buyer and their individual motivations. You have to configure solutions, establish your credibility, identify the antagonists, enamor yourself to influencers, discover where the competition is falling short, and do all the other things professional salespeople ought to do. But you need to do all of these things long before the RFP is issued.

Put bluntly, you need to start selling.

CHAPTER RECAP

You cannot wait for an RFP to fall in your lap and then reasonably expect you have a chance at winning. You don't.

If you want to win more RFPs, more consistently, you must be proactive. Instead of asking, "how do we win this RFP?" that just came in the door, you should be saying, "I want to win this contract when it goes out to bid in three years, *and here's how we are going to do it!*"

Part 1: Proposal Writing Best Practices

3. Focus on the Buyer, not the Seller

As we launch into our discussion of proposal writing best practices, we begin with what is the most fundamental best practice of all—focusing on the needs of the buyer. We should be talking about them, not about us.

Unfortunately, this is the first place where most proposals fall short.

THE COMMON PRACTICE—TALK ABOUT YOURSELF

If you meet someone at a cocktail party, would you immediately begin talking about yourself? Would you launch a conversation with, "Hi, I'm Dave. Let me tell you about me?" Of course you wouldn't! It's a surefire way to drive people away. It makes you sound self-centered and arrogant.

Even though most of us understand this basic rule of social discourse, it's almost routine for many sellers to begin their proposals with a letter or executive summary that does exactly this. I review many proposals every year. Even though I should be used to it by now, I am continually astonished by how much sellers talk about themselves. Us, we, me. Us, we, me.

While I was drafting this chapter, I got a call from a potential client asking me to review a proposal he had written. Over the first five pages, I observed that every paragraph began with either his company's name or a pronoun such as "we" or "our." Every one. Clearly, this seller wasn't focused on the needs of the client, he was focused on himself and telling his company's story.

It's easy to understand why this happens. When a buyer sends an RFP that includes 50 or 100 questions asking about your company and your product, the natural inclination is to respond with lots of information. In fact, I was onsite with one client when she shared their company philosophy about writing proposals:

> They send us an RFP because they want to know about us, so we tell them. Everything.

Like I said, it's easy to understand why this is a common practice. Still, it's a horrible way to write a proposal.

WHY THE COMMON PRACTICE IS A WORST PRACTICE

Focusing on yourself more than the buyer may be common, but it's a worst practice, not a best practice. Here's why.

Buyers want to know about you. It's why they send you an RFP. But it's important to recognize they only want to know about you within the context of how *you are going to help them get what they want*. They want to know how you are going to use your products and services and people and resources to solve their problems.

When your proposal content focuses on you more than the buyer, you aren't telling them what's in it for them. When all you're doing is sharing pages and pages of information about your company, your products, and how many awards you've won, you aren't telling them what's in it for them. It's a problem because when all you're doing is talking about yourself, you aren't saying those magic, all-important words all buyers want to hear: "And here's what this means to you…"

It's not about you, it's about them.

EXERCISE: CRITIQUING YOUR OWN PROPOSALS

Take a moment and find one or two recent proposals your company submitted, including the cover letters that accompanied them. Generally, it's best if it wasn't a proposal you wrote personally or spent time reviewing; you may be too close to be able to review it objectively. Either way, browse through the proposal and ask yourself this one critical question:

Is this proposal more about your company or the buyer?

One of the techniques I use during this exercise is to look at the first word of each paragraph. I do this because it's a quick tell. Do most of these paragraphs begin with your company name? Or pronouns like *we* and *our*?

- *Dave's Fictional Coffee Cups is pleased to…*
- *We strive to be…*
- *Our team has built a customer services program…*
- *When building our program, we made certain to…*

See the point? None of these sentences is focused on the client and what they want, they're focused on you. Us, we, me. Us, we, me. You're talking about yourself, but you aren't telling them *what's in it for them.*

It can be humbling to critique one of your own proposals against some objective standard, but if you keep an open mind, it's almost always enlightening.

THE BEST PRACTICE—FOCUS ON THE BUYER

When you are writing a proposal, one of the most important of all best practices is to talk about the buyer, not about you. You need to focus on their issues and challenges, their goals and objectives. Even when you're talking about you, you have to find a way to make it about them. Even when you're answering a simple question about how many years you've been in business, you have to structure your response so it addresses the things they are most concerned about. *It's not about you, it's about them.*

Making it about them by using benefit statements

One of the easiest ways I've found to 'make it about them' is to include benefit statements in your answers. A benefit statement is little more than an explanation, included at key points throughout your proposal, that helps the buyer understand the advantage or benefit they receive.

- *And here's what this means to you…*
- *What this means to you is…*
- *The benefit of this approach to you is…*

- *This approach offers many advantages for your staff. First...*

Including benefit statements in your writing is so easy, but it's also an effective way to make your writing focused on the buyer.

In this example, the following paragraph is what many writers might include if they were drafting a payroll services proposal:

> *The payroll processing solution we are proposing includes payroll cards. Payroll cards are like debit cards. Each pay period, we are able to transfer a person's pay directly to their payroll card.*

Now see how it changes if you add a benefit statement that describes the benefit they, or in this case their employees, will receive:

> *Payroll cards are an important benefit for your hourly employees at your Cleveland manufacturing facility, many of whom do not have personal checking accounts. Instead of being forced to pay a hefty fee to cash a paper check, a common practice, the payroll card gives these employees immediate and full access to their earnings free of fees. They get to keep more of their money.*

Again, it's a simple thing to add this benefit statement at the end of your answer, but it goes a long way to ensure your content is focused on the buyer instead of yourself.

If you do nothing else, if you take away no other advice from this book, finishing each answer with a simple benefit statement will dramatically improve the effectiveness of your proposal content.

Making it about them by rewriting stock answers

Including benefit statements is important and easy to do, but for the really important answers, you should consider rewriting your content to make your entire response about them. Following are some examples that demonstrate how you can make even stock, boring content more focused on the buyer and their needs.

Example #1—Re-writing a stock answer so it is about them

Suppose you discover the buyer's last two vendors were both small startups that went out of business halfway through the contract. Suppose you also learn the buyer is anxious about choosing a new vendor because they don't want the same thing to happen again. Clearly, this is an important piece of sales intelligence, and assuming you are an established company with staying power, it's an important differentiator, too. You need to highlight it. Unfortunately, too many writers miss the opportunity. When asked how long you've been in business, many proposal writers would respond with a simple, informative answer.

Q: How long have you been in business?

A. We've been in business since 1981.

This answer is compliant, to be sure, but it does nothing to address the buyer's main concern. And don't forget, though it's important to be compliant, our mission is to make a sale.

As an alternative, consider reworking this stock answer to focus on some of the things you know they are concerned about, such as the likelihood your company will be around tomorrow.

Q: How long have you been in business?

A. Our coffee cup company is an established organization in business since 1981. Over the past ten years, in particular, we have maintained a manageable and sustainable 10% annual growth rate.

You can be confident we have the organizational and financial stability— the staying power—so you won't have to go searching for a new coffee cup vendor before the current contract term ends.

See the difference? Most proposal writers would answer this question with the simple, informational answer. But when you turn it around to focus on what they care about most—vendor stability—you made it meaningful to them. You made it substantive. *It's not about you, it's about them.*

Example #2—Re-writing a stock answer so it is about them

Suppose you learn your buyer is struggling to find a vendor who is more responsive and attentive to their needs than their current vendor. Despite having this insight, too many writers miss simple opportunities to address this kind of requirement. For example, when asked how many offices they have, most proposal writers would respond with a simple, informative answer.

Q. How many offices do you have?

A. We have 54 offices.

Like the previous example, this answer is accurate and compliant. The problem is it does nothing to address the buyer's main concern.

As an alternative, consider this example in which we draw a parallel between where *your* offices are located against where *their* offices are located. Then we make the point that because of your close geographic proximity, your company will be more responsive and quick to respond.

Q. How many offices do you have?

A. We have 54 offices located throughout the United States. Further, we mapped the locations of your offices and we compared that to a map of our own office locations. Based on this analysis, we determined that we have an office located within ten miles of 90% of your facilities, and 100% of your largest facilities.

This means we have the resources, in place today, to respond quickly whenever your staff requires our services.

Clearly, this customer-focused answer is longer and requires more effort than a simple informational answer, but given what you know about the buyer, which one is going to be more effective? Which one will help you win the sale? *It's not about you, it's about them.*

CHAPTER RECAP

The single biggest mistake most proposal writers make is they talk about themselves. It's certainly understandable; when a buyer sends you an RFP filled with 50, 75, or a 100 questions asking about your product and your company, the natural inclination is to write answers that are all about you. But buyers don't want to know about you, not really. They want to know how you are going to use your capabilities to help them get what they want.

Sellers must remember it's not about you, it's about them, so even when you're talking about you, you have to find a way to make it about them.

4. Write to Persuade, Not to Inform

Whenever I'm talking with a new client and advocate the importance of communicating persuasively, almost everyone agrees. In fact, someone almost always says something like, "We do that, already." When I look at the proposals they've written, though, it's clear they do not do that already.

In most cases, they aren't communicating persuasively, they're communicating informatively; they're throwing lots and lots of information against the wall and hoping something sticks.

Therefore, before we go any further, it's important we discuss what is meant by, "communicating persuasively."

PEOPLE COMMUNICATE FOR THREE BASIC REASONS

In a business setting, people generally communicate for one of three reasons; to inform, to explain, or to persuade.

Communicating to inform

When you communicate to inform, all you're doing is sharing facts:
- *This car has antilock brakes.*
- *The lunchroom is painted green.*
- *That copier has an advance phase plutomatic core.*

You aren't saying whether the fact you share is good or bad, preferable or something to avoid, you aren't even explaining what it means. All you're doing is sharing the fact.

Inherent in this fact-sharing approach is an assumption that the buyer will understand the fact you share, what it means, and why it's important to him or her. That's a big assumption, though, and one that's not always borne out by reality. Consider the following example.

I was working for a software company that sold school administration and grade tracking software to secondary schools. They believed their target audience was senior school administrators, skilled professionals who had advanced degrees not just in education but also in school administration. Therefore, their proposals used lots of terms and concepts that this audience would understand and appreciate. The problem, we came to find out, was they had the wrong audience. In fact, the people who reviewed their proposals were typically heterogeneous committees made up of teachers, front office secretaries, back office staff, parents and PTA members, the occasional lunch lady, and a bunch of other people who work or volunteer at the school. The problem is these people couldn't fully appreciate the message we were trying to communicate because there were so many parts they didn't understand. My client was writing to the wrong audience.

This is not a unique occurrence.

Many state and local government procurement programs routinely conscript proposal reviewers from departments other than the department involved in the procurement. Procurement staff sometimes does this because they don't want the current staff to just rubber stamp the incumbent vendor. They think drafting people from other departments will promote objectivity and ensure a competitive procurement. The problem, of course, is the staff from the other departments don't always understand the complexities or subtleties of the product or service being acquired. If you bring in Sally from accounting to evaluate a road improvement proposal, do you really think she's going to understand half of what she reads?

Therefore, while communicating to inform is a great way to efficiently share information among equally knowledgeable people, it's a horrible approach in a proposal because, often as not, your reviewers don't always understand the significance of what you're trying to say.

Communicating to explain

When you communicate to explain, you go one step further. In addition to sharing the fact, you also explain its significance:

- *This car has antilock brakes. Antilock brakes help the driver maintain control while braking in slippery driving conditions.*
- *This copier has an advance phase plutomatic core. This innovative device will double the copier's operational life while reducing maintenance costs by half.*

Communicating to explain acknowledges that everyone reading your proposal may not understand the significance of every fact you share or every term you employ. This is important because, like in the previous school software example, your proposal may be reviewed by people who do not fully understand what you are selling.

Here's one more example, because this topic is that important. When it comes to local government procurements—counties, cities, etc.—the people who make the final decisions about major public procurements are often local elected officials. The reason this is notable is because these local-level elected officials are often professionals in other areas. The mayor may be a real estate professional, for example, or a professor at the local college. Council members may be a conglomeration of lawyers, local community activists, business people, doctors, educators, merchants, etc. If they're reviewing your proposal, and you don't explain every idea you state, many of them likely won't understand the significance of what you're trying to articulate.

The point is unless you explain things fully, you cannot be confident the people evaluating your proposals will fully understand what's being proposed.

> Communicating to explain is the method to use when your audience does not necessarily understand the significance or meaning of the fact you are sharing. And that's almost 100% of the time.

Communicating to persuade

When we communicate to persuade, we're going one step further. We aren't just sharing information or explanations, we're actually recommending that one thing, method, or approach is preferable to or better than another:

"I recommend you buy this car because it has antilock brakes. You said your daughter is learning to drive, and you want a car that is safe. Antilock brakes will help her to maintain control in slippery driving conditions. Therefore, I recommend you buy this car for your daughter because it's safer than that car over there."

Communicating to persuade is the most challenging kind of communication. When we communicate to persuade, we don't just provide information to the reader and hope they come to the correct conclusion, we're taking them by the hand and walking them down the path. We're guiding them turn by turn, decision by decision around each obstacle, and ultimately, we're leading them to the correct conclusion.

> Communicating to persuade is the method to use when you are trying to convince your audience to choose a particular path or make a particular decision.

WHY IS IT IMPORTANT TO COMMUNICATE PERSUASIVELY?

I was teaching a seminar when a lady asked this question. I hesitated because I didn't know what to say. Up to that point, I assumed everyone understood the ability to persuade is a necessary skill in the business development world. The more I considered her question, though, the more I came to realize it was a good question. Here's why.

I came to the proposal field from a background in sales and business development. I'd been a sales person with a territory and a quota, I'd been a sales manager, and I'd been in other business development roles. Because of this experience, I already understood that persuasive communication is a tool as fundamental to sellers as a hammer to a carpenter and a pipe wrench to a plumber.

In contrast, many people do not arrive in the proposal writing profession with a business development background. Some were administrative assistants or specialists and were drafted into the proposal development effort. Many more were marketing people who lent their help to a proposal effort, did an OK job, and then found themselves conscripted onto the proposal development team. Still others were subject matter experts (SMEs) who demonstrated the unique and highly coveted ability to articulate technical topics in ways that other, non-technical people can understand. When a proposal team finds an SME with this kind of talent, they don't ever let go.

> Many people who are involved in the proposal development effort got there through decidedly circuitous routes. As a result, many do not have a business development background, and therefore, many do not understand or fully appreciate the importance of communicating persuasively.

As we launch into this discussion, therefore, we need to begin by answering the lady's question: *"Why is it important to communicate persuasively?"*

It's important to communicate persuasively anytime we want someone else to make a decision a certain way, do something we believe they should do, or in our case, buy the product we are selling. Politicians try to persuade us they are the most qualified candidates, fast food restaurants try to persuade us they have the juiciest hamburgers or the tastiest fries, parents try to persuade their kids to avoid drugs and get good grades—you get the idea.

Sometimes, you have influence over other people. This means you hold some leverage over them that gives you the ability to more or less "force" a particular action. If you're a manager, you have some level of authority, and therefore influence, over the people who report to you. If you're a parent, you have some level of authority, and therefore influence, over your kids. The boss can say, "you will do your work according to this process (if you hope to keep working at this company)." The parent can say, "you will eat your vegetables (if you want that new toy so badly)." They have the authority that gives them influence, that allows them to impose a specific action.

The problem is if someone is doing something because he has to, and not because he wants to, it's unlikely he'll do it well. It's even less likely he'll continue doing it after the force is removed or fades away. Sure, your kid eats her Brussels sprouts tonight while you're making her, while you're watching. But unless she actually wants to eat them, then the moment you aren't looking she feeds them to the dog (who doesn't eat them, either, but that's another issue). In other words, force is not a good way to change behavior. *The best way to change behavior is to change the attitudes that influence the behavior.* And this, in a nutshell, is why it's important to communicate persuasively.

Persuasion is about changing someone's behavior by first changing their attitudes. We aren't *making* them do something, or even *tricking* them into doing something, we're demonstrating to them, convincing them, that what we propose is in their best interest. If the other person agrees what we propose is in their best interest, they're more likely to choose the decision path we are proposing.

So how do we convince them? By building persuasively structured arguments that clearly and rationally explain why the solution we are proposing is the best choice for them.

How to communicate persuasively

Accepting it's important to communicate persuasively, the next logical question is, *"how* do you do that...*how* do you communicate persuasively?"* It's a good question, to be sure, but it's a little bit like asking, "what is the meaning of life?" It's a little question with a really big answer.

For our purposes in this book, we don't have enough time or space to explore persuasive theory in all its extensive complexity. Instead, what I try to do here is to boil down all the theory into a repeatable technique for building persuasively structured arguments.

Building persuasively structured arguments

When your goal is to persuade someone, you don't just throw a bunch of information at the reader and hope they come to the correct conclusion. Instead, you build a structured argument. The structured argument you build takes them by the hand and walks them down the correct path, step by step, point by point, until you reach the correct conclusion together.

If you are wrongly accused of a crime, and you hire a lawyer to represent you, your lawyer is not going to present a bunch of information and then hope the jury comes to the correct decision. If your lawyer is any good at all, he or she is going to present a structured argument that proactively leads the jury down the path to the correct conclusion.

> *Ladies and gentlemen of the jury, my client is innocent...and I can prove it!*
>
> *This horrible crime occurred on Saturday at 9:05 a.m. My client could not have committed this crime because when it happened, he was all the way across town—17 miles away—taking money out of an ATM machine.*
>
> *As evidence to support this claim, here is the ATM receipt with a time stamp for exactly 9:05, along with a picture, taken by the ATM, that clearly shows it was my client who was withdrawing the money.*
>
> *I understand the prosecution has introduced an eye witness placing my client at the scene of the crime, and for what it's worth, I believe the witness, Mr. Smith, is doing his best to faithfully recall the events as they happened. Still, every expert will tell you that eye witness testimony is not dependable.*
>
> *What is dependable is an ATM time stamp and a photograph. So even though Mr. Smith thinks he saw my client at the scene of the crime, the photograph and ATM time stamp PROVE otherwise.*
>
> *Therefore, ladies and gentlemen of the jury, you must conclude that my client is innocent because he was on the other side of town when this crime occurred.*

Though relatively simplistic, this is an excellent example of how to build a persuasively structured argument. The attorney doesn't take any chances that the audience (jury) might come to an incorrect conclusion, she leads them to the correct conclusion. First, she makes her statement, "my client is innocent." Then, step by step, point by point, she explains why she's able to make that claim. She also provides evidence to support it. Finally, she draws a conclusion—the *only* logical conclusion that can be drawn from the argument and evidence presented.

Whether you're a lawyer arguing the innocence of your client or a seller trying to make a sale, you rely on the same structured, methodical approach.

HOW TO STRUCTURE PERSUASIVE ARGUMENTS

For our purposes writing proposal content, there are five parts to writing a persuasive argument.

1. Make a statement, a claim, or a recommendation.
2. Make your argument, and include any explanation that is necessary.
3. Provide evidence to support your claim.
4. Acknowledge and address alternative views.
5. Conclude your argument.

Let's explore each of these in greater detail.

1. Make a statement, a claim, or a recommendation

The way to begin building a persuasive argument is to make a statement, a claim, or a recommendation so the reader knows what you're talking about. In the previous example, our capable attorney begins with a claim so straightforward there's no ambiguity about the argument she's making:

> "Ladies and gentlemen of the jury, my client is innocent…and I can prove it!"

We need to take the same, straightforward approach when writing proposal content. Suppose we're selling a fictional office copier, we might begin our discussion with something like this:

> In your RFP, you stated you want an office copier that has better reliability and reduced maintenance costs. We recommend you purchase the OfficeRocket 3000 because it delivers both.

Like our legal example above, this claim is so clear and straightforward there is no ambiguity; the reader knows exactly what we are proposing and why.

There's something else that's very important in this statement; we're actually making a recommendation. We aren't minimizing our offering by using "wishy washy" language that says something like, "please consider our copier." We're increasing the persuasiveness of our statement by making a firm and clear recommendation. If you've established credibility with the decision makers in the buying organization, making a recommendation in this way is, by itself, persuasive.

2. Make your argument, and include any explanation that is necessary.

In our legal eagle example above, our intrepid attorney builds a concise argument which includes a clear explanation why her client is innocent:

> *This horrible crime occurred on Saturday at 9:05 a.m. My client could not have committed this crime because when it happened, he was all the way across town—17 miles away—taking money out of an ATM machine.*

As proposal writers, we must take the same approach. We began by making a claim—or in this case a recommendation. Now we have to explain it so the buyer understands why our recommendation delivers what they want.

> *The OfficeRocket 3000 is constructed with our patented 'reverse phase plutomatic core.' This innovative, new technology reduces the number of moving parts by half. Not only does this reduce regular maintenance by half, it effectively doubles the lifespan you can expect from your copier.*

This short paragraph is marvelous because any buyer who reads it, even someone who knows nothing about office copier technology, will immediately understand the significance of the statement.

3. Provide evidence to support your claim.

If I told you the moon is made of cheese, even if I explained why I thought it is so, you'd likely be skeptical...and for good reason! You can't just tell someone "the moon is made of cheese," and then expect them to believe you. You can't just say "we've got great customer service," and then expect them to believe you.

If you want people to believe you, you have to provide proof to support your claims. The good news is there are multiple kinds of evidence you can rely on to support the claims you make.

- Documented facts from an independent, objective source
- An opinion from an independent, objective source

- Quotes from other customers
- Mini case studies from other customers
- Past performance statistics
- Relevant awards you've won
- Audience experience

Let's explore.

Documented facts from an independent, objective source

If you say, "my client is innocent because he was across town when this crime occurred," you must provide proof to support the claim that he was, in fact, across town.

> As evidence to support this claim, here is the ATM receipt with a time stamp for exactly 9:05, along with a picture, taken by the ATM, that clearly shows it was my client who was withdrawing the money.

A documented fact from an objective, independent source—in this case a time stamped ATM receipt and photograph—is one of the best kinds of evidence you can use to support your claims. It's so effective because it truly is objective; no one can reasonably argue the ATM is biased for or against the defendant.

An opinion from an independent, objective source

An objective opinion or assessment from a reputable organization is nearly as effective as an objective fact, and can still be a great way to prove an argument:

> This last June, the Fictional Office Copier Testing Association reported its findings after a year-long "torture test" of the top ten office copiers on the market today. Their findings support our claims. Specifically, they found the OfficeRocket 3000 required half the maintenance of the other copiers, and based on engineering analysis, is projected to last twice as long as the other machines tested.

It's an opinion, so it is inherently subjective. Still, it's a subjective conclusion from an objective source, so it has lots of credibility.

Quotes from other customers

Another kind of evidence that is more subjective but still highly effective is a quote from an existing customer. These quotes aren't as objective as a statement or finding from an independent, professional organization, but they can often be even more influential because they come from people who have already bought the same product or service.

> *"We use our copier all the time, but with our old copier, we were getting frustrated at the high maintenance costs and how frequently it had to be repaired. Then we found the OfficeRocket 3000. It's consistently reliable, maintenance costs are low, and it just keeps going. We couldn't be more pleased." -Albert Jones, Office Manager*

In his book, *Influence,* Robert Cialdini discusses the power of what we commonly refer to as 'peer pressure.'[1] He explains the phenomena is just as profound among adults as it is with school kids. So what does that mean for proposal writers?

If you're the office manager and you've been struggling with an office copier that breaks down constantly, you're likely to find the quote from Albert Jones compelling. It's from another office manager just like you, and he's dealing with the exact same problem you are. Further, the outcome he got is the same outcome you want.

Peer pressure isn't just for kids anymore.

Mini case studies from other customers

In the same way quotes from other customers can be used as evidence to support a persuasive argument, mini case studies about other customers are also effective. They're effective because they give the buyer the opportunity to visualize your product in a setting like theirs.

A mini case study is only three paragraphs. The first paragraph should outline the problem. The second paragraph should document the solution. The third paragraph should describe the outcome the buyer received.

---

[1] *I highly recommend all proposal writers and business development professionals read Influence by Cialdini.*

You can insert your case study into your content, but I generally recommend including it in a callout box. It stands out from the text and encourages people who are skimming your proposal to read it.

How the OfficeRocket 3000 is Saving Money and Reducing Downtime for Office Managers

Office managers have many responsibilities, one of which is making sure the office has all of the office equipment it needs to function well. As Albert Jones knows too well, this can be a problem if your office copier is constantly breaking.

After evaluating many alternatives, Albert Jones replaced their previous copier with the Office Rocket 3000. Extensive industry "torture testing" proved its reliability, and clinched Albert's decision. Before long, he knew it was the *correct* decision.

"We couldn't be more pleased," said Albert. "The Office Rocket 3000 is reliable. In fact, it hasn't faltered once in the six months since we installed it."

Wherever you put it, mini case studies are an excellent kind of evidence for topics that are traditionally difficult-to-prove like customer service quality, the effectiveness of your quality program, etc.

Past performance statistics

Many companies keep statistics about their performance. For example, a company that fields incoming phone calls from consumers may track statistics such as these:

- How long it takes before a consumer is connected to an agent.
- How many times a consumer hangs up before being connected to an agent.
- How many times the agent can answer the question on the first call vs. escalating the call to a more senior person.

These kinds of performance statistics are subjective in the sense the company is self-reporting, but they can still be effective if you demonstrate a disciplined approach to collecting and maintaining the data.

Awards

Awards you've won can be an effective kind of evidence, but only if used wisely. I say it this way because many proposal writers will look for an opportunity to list all of their awards in one section. This approach doesn't help.

The correct way to use awards effectively is to present them as evidence within the context of an answer to a relevant question. For example, if you are answering a question about your company's hiring practices for disabled or disadvantaged people, the first thing you do is to answer the question by listing your hiring practices. Then, as evidence of your commitment to the program, you can list the awards you've received from various organizations that recognize your effort in this area.

Try not to list awards that are over a few years old. A five-year-old award, no matter how awesome it was when you received it, is less than compelling.

Appealing to Audience experience

Persuasion does not always require changing the buyer's way of thinking. Sometimes, their thinking, their views, are already in line with yours. In these cases, persuading them to decide a certain way only requires demonstrating how their approach and your approach are already aligned.

One of my long-time clients is unique in their market. While most of the vendors use the same or similar methods to provide their services, my client has used truly innovative methods to improve both the effectiveness and efficiency of their service. In certain service lines, they could literally do twice the work in half the time with far greater accuracy.

When one of our senior salespeople approached a buyer, the buyer made clear he didn't want to hear another presentation pitching the same old tired methods; he would only listen if we were using innovative methods that would dramatically improve the results. Our sales rep immediately aligned our commitment to innovative methods to the buyer's singular interest in innovative methods. We had his attention.

The point is we didn't have to change his mind that an innovative and automated process was better, all we had to do was to convince him that we were already in agreement.

If you want people to believe you, to accept your arguments, you have to provide proof—*evidence*—to support your claims. Good evidence makes your persuasive arguments credible and meaningful.

4. Acknowledge and address alternative views.

When someone is trying to make a decision, and there are two or more people with differing arguments, the person has to evaluate both and decide which one he finds more compelling. And don't forget, in most procurements, there are usually more than one decision maker. This is why it is sometimes necessary for a seller to acknowledge the other side's argument and explain either what's wrong with it or why it is not as good as yours.

> *Ladies and gentlemen of the jury, I understand the prosecution has introduced an eye witness placing my client at the scene of the crime. And for what it's worth, I believe the witness, Mr. Smith, is doing his best to faithfully recall the events as they happened. Still, every expert in law enforcement will tell you that eye witness testimony is not universally dependable. What is dependable is an ATM time stamp and a photograph. So even though Mr. Smith thinks he saw my client at the scene of the crime, the photograph and ATM time stamp PROVE otherwise.*

This is an effective way to handle a competing argument. Not only do we acknowledge the other side's argument, we also acknowledge that they are not purposefully being dishonest—*Mr. Smith is doing his best to faithfully recall the events as they happened.* But then we clarify why his testimony is unreliable and why ours isn't.

We need to use the same kind of approach when writing our office copier argument.

> *We understand other office copier manufacturers continue to claim the "core-free" copier engine is better because it's been around so long, because it's proven. It is true the core-free design has been around a long*

time and is proven. In fact, it's the same design we used exclusively for many years.

Despite this, after discovering the many advantages of the reverse-phase plutomatic core, and after extensive testing proved the new core was far better and more reliable than the core-free design, we made the investment to retool our manufacturing facilities to embrace this better system.

It's important to be careful when challenging a competitor's argument. You don't want to sound overly negative or arrogant, and you definitely don't want to say anything negative about a product or service the customer has already purchased; that will do little more than put them on the defensive. Also, you almost never want to call out a competitor by name. This can reflect poorly on you and potentially open you up to legal issues.

Despite all this, you can't ignore their arguments. You have to confront them and you have to undermine their relevance. Carefully, deliberately, you must make certain the reader understands why the competitor's argument is flawed and yours is preferable.

To be clear, proposal answers do not always require alternative views. Sometimes they aren't necessary, other times you don't know what the alternative view is, etc. If it makes sense, include it. If it doesn't, don't.

5. Conclude your argument.

When learning to speak in public, aspiring orators are often given this advice:

Tell them what you're going to tell them, tell them, and then tell them what you told them.

People absorb new ideas at different rates. Some remarkable people are able to absorb new ideas quickly and incorporate them into their thinking straightaway. For the rest of us, it takes more time to process all of the new information we're receiving. The three-step approach described above makes it easier for most of us to process a new message so we can then incorporate it more easily into our thinking.

In building our argument so far, we've already done two of the three steps; we told them what we're going to tell them and then we told them. Now, we have to wrap it up by reiterating what we've already told them.

> *Therefore, ladies and gentlemen of the jury, you must conclude that my client is innocent because he was on the other side of town when this crime occurred.*

This final statement is like the ribbon on a birthday present; it wraps up the entire argument into a nice and neat little package. As proposal writers, we want to do the exact same thing, but with one caveat. We also want to add some verbiage that explains that the buyer is going to get everything they said they want.

> *By choosing the OfficeRocket 3000, you will get everything you said you wanted in a new office copier—reduced maintenance and longer life—and both of these translate into better copier reliability and reduced costs over the life of the machine.*

When trying to persuade someone else, it's always critical to remind them, at the end of the argument, "what's in it for them." Especially in long proposal answers where it's easy to get lost in all the details, wrapping it up with a benefit statement is a requirement. This is precisely why I always try to wrap up answers to RFP questions with something like this:

> *"The advantage of this approach is…"*

> *"What this means to you is…"*

> *"This approach offers many benefits, but one of the most important is…"*

> *"The benefit of this approach is…"*

Being persuasive necessarily means making it about the buyer and what they want. Therefore, finishing every argument by refocusing on them—and especially what's in it for them—is critical.

HOW TO WRITE PERSUASIVELY—A FEW EXAMPLES

Examples are a great tool for proposal writers and, coincidentally, people writing books about proposals. They take something conceptual and make it real and understandable. Here are a couple examples to help you understand.

Example #1 — The OfficeRocket 3000 example presented together

Over the previous pages, we used snippets from a larger argument built to answer the RFP question, *"Describe how your solution will provide us with better office copier reliability, reduced maintenance, and a longer useful life."* Following are all of those snippets combined so you can see how it all fits together.

In your RFP, you stated you want an office copier that has better reliability and reduced maintenance costs. We recommend you purchase the OfficeRocket 3000 because it delivers both.

Better reliability, reduced maintenance

The OfficeRocket 3000 is constructed with our patented 'reverse phase plutomatic core.' This innovative, new technology reduces the number of moving parts by half. Not only does this reduce regular maintenance by half, it effectively doubles the lifespan you can expect from your copier.

"We use our copier all the time, but we were getting frustrated at the high maintenance costs and how frequently it needed repairs. It wasn't reliable. Then we found the OfficeRocket 3000. It's consistently reliable, maintenance costs are low, and it just keeps going. We couldn't be more pleased."

Albert Jones

Objective proof

This last June, the Fictional Office Copier Testing Association reported its findings after a year-long "torture test" of the top ten office copiers on the market today. Their findings support our claims. Specifically, they found the OfficeRocket 3000 required half the maintenance of the other copiers, and based on engineering analysis, it is projected to last twice as long as the other machines tested.

Old tech is...old

We understand other office copier manufacturers continue to claim the "core-free" copier engine is better because it's been around so long, because it's proven. It is true the core-free design has been around a long time and is proven. In fact, it's the same design we used exclusively for many years.

Despite this, after discovering the many advantages of the reverse-phase plutomatic core, and after extensive testing proved the new core was far better and more reliable than the core-free design, we made the investment to retool our manufacturing facilities to embrace this better system.

Outcome? Better reliability and reduced maintenance

By choosing the OfficeRocket 3000, you will get everything you said you wanted in a new office copier—better reliability, reduced maintenance, and a longer operational life.

Example #2—a persuasively structured customer service answer

In an RFP, customer service questions are always the most difficult to answer. This is because every seller claims to provide great customer service—*and who wouldn't?* The problem is "good customer service" is a concept so intangible it's difficult to demonstrate or prove. This example demonstrates how you might build a persuasively structured argument that shows your excellent customer service.

Background

The Buyer had been working with its current payroll processing vendor for most of the previous ten years. Everything was great. But then their current vendor's ownership changed and, when it did, service levels declined. Today, if they call their vendor, an associate isn't always available. When they do get a call back, it's often delayed by a day or more and the response is not always helpful. It doesn't help calling management either. It's as if the new ownership scaled back on staff so much there's no one available or able to help.

RFP question

Please describe your customer service program, customer service response times, and escalation procedures if we do not receive targeted service levels.

The persuasively structured answer

If one of your staff has a question that needs answering or an issue that needs resolving, you shouldn't have to wait for help. You expect your payroll vendor to be available and to respond quickly. At Dave's Fictional Payroll Processing Company, we do.

Personal service = better outcomes

In building this program for you, we designed a client service team arrangement that matches each of your office managers to the senior manager at each of our closest office locations. In other words, your staff never calls into a customer service call center, they call a person they already know at their local Dave's Payroll office. If the senior manager is not there, there is always a secondary contact available to help.

Every payroll provider claims to provide great customer service, but Dave's actually delivers. We couldn't be more pleased, and we wouldn't hesitate to recommend them if you're looking for payroll services.

This arrangement, built around close proximity and personal relationships, produces better outcomes. You get more attentive service from someone you know and who knows you, and you never have to wait more than an hour to get a call back. In fact, an hour is the outside exception, not the rule.

Escalation procedures to eliminate frustration

Between your primary, day-to-day contact and easy access to the local office manager, all of your staff across your entire organization will receive attentive and responsive service.

Still, if one of your office staff is ever dissatisfied with the service they are receiving from the local account team member, he or she can contact Bob

Jones. Bob is the senior account manager working with your headquarters office, and is responsible for the performance of the entire account team. Bob's job is to ensure your staff is happy with our service, and if they aren't, he has the motivation—and the authority—to make it right.

Delivering quality customer service

The solution we are proposing—built around personal relationships and close proximity—may be unique in the industry, but it delivers exactly the kind of responsive service you want. You can be confident your staff will never again have to wait for an answer to a question or a resolution to a problem.

The preceding example is fictional, and realistically, it is shorter than most answers you will typically write when responding to an important RFP question. Still, contrast this very customer-focused and persuasive answer against the typical, longer, information-laden, stock answer that most writers would "plug in" to answer the same question.

In the real world, I would work to find more specifics to present. I would search for proof—performance statistics, for example—that I could share to support the contention that our personal approach works better. Here are a few examples of things I'd consider adding to this answer.

- Include a list of your office managers and office assistants who would be assigned to each of their offices. You might even include a brief background on each manager.
- Include statistics that document how long it takes today for existing customers to get through to the assigned office manager on the first call.
- Include statistics that document how long it takes for existing customers today to get a call back if the office manager is not available.

Much of this is information you are probably already including in your proposals somewhere, but recognize it's just that…information. You don't always know how your customers are going to interpret it. When you put this information in the context of a structured argument, though, where you first acknowledge their issues and then wrap it up by reminding them the benefit they'll receive, the evidence becomes a lot more meaningful and compelling for them.

CHAPTER RECAP

Most proposal writers are most comfortable providing informational answers, but remember your goal is not to share information, it's to make a sale. This means you have to transition from just sharing information to building a persuasive reason why they should choose you and the solution you are proposing.

If all you're doing is sharing information, you don't always know if the reviewer will understand its significance. If you put all of your information within the context of a persuasive argument, however, you're helping them come to the correct conclusion.

There are five things you need to do to build a persuasive argument.

1. Make a statement, a claim, or a recommendation.
2. Make your argument, and include any explanation that is necessary.
3. Provide evidence to support your claim.
4. Acknowledge and address alternative views.
5. Conclude your argument.

5. Sell to People, Not Organizations

In all of my years as a professional salesperson, I have never once encountered a situation where a purchase decision was made by an organization. Every purchase decision I've been involved in—every single one—was made by a person. Admittedly, this short introduction may seem like I'm playing word games but I'm not and here's why.

When you receive an RFP, it usually articulates the objectives the organization wants to achieve or the problems they want to resolve. But as sellers, we need to recognize that these objectives are nothing more than the expression of an individual decision maker's personal motivation or concern—appropriately formalized and sanitized into corporate speak.

> Personal motivations drive organizational objectives. Discover the motivation and you'll understand the objective.

Consider this example. The new VP of Sales was getting ready to visit a client to close his first major sale, but he couldn't complete the trip because his company car wouldn't start. He came to learn it wasn't the first time this car (that he inherited from the previous VP) had the same problem. He also learned that two other sales reps had experienced the same problem twice. Therefore, when the company later issued an RFP to replace their current fleet, they included a requirement that the new cars be reliable.

When we put this into context, what we have is a personal motivation that's powerful and actionable, but it's driving an organizational objective that is, at best, generic:

- **Personal motivation**: *I almost lost a major sale, the first big sale since I've been in my new position, because my car wouldn't start.*
- **Organizational objective as articulated in the RFP**: *We require cars that are reliable.*

See the difference? As a proposal writer, as a salesperson who writes on paper, I can do a great job writing to the first point because it's specific and actionable. I can build a buyer-focused argument that acknowledges the issue the VP of Sales articulates, and explain the specific parts of our solution that prevent the same thing from ever happening again.

I can't do the same with the second point. The second point is so generic all I can do is respond with a solution that is equally generic: "our cars are reliable."

COMMON PRACTICE = SELL TO ORGANIZATIONS, NOT PEOPLE

The problem is that most of the proposals that sellers write today are to organizations, not the people who work there. They're really good at addressing the generic organizational objectives and requirements listed in RFPs, but they often fail to address the motivations of the individuals, the people, who are making the decisions.

We need to change this.

BEST PRACTICE = FOCUS ON THE PEOPLE

In the previous chapter, we discussed how dad is looking for a safe car to buy for his daughter as she learns how to drive. This is good information to begin with, but what's the motivation behind his interest in safety? Sure, all parents want their kids to be safe, but is there something more?

Suppose we discover dad's oldest son was in a wreck when he was learning how to drive and was in the hospital for two weeks recovering. Dad never wants to go through anything like that again. So now that his daughter is getting ready to drive, he becomes very protective. *This is his motivation.*

As a proposal writer, you can't always use personal motivations directly when creating proposal content. Still, knowing the buyer's motivation, knowing the story behind the requirements, you could craft a buyer-focused proposal that addresses exactly the things dad really cares about:

> *Look Mr. Dad, I think I get it. Your daughter is learning to drive. You want her to be safe. It's an issue because so many cars these days are smaller and just don't provide the protection of a bigger vehicle where the occupants are surrounded and protected by a sturdy structure. With these smaller cars, even small accidents can result in injuries.*

> *Nothing is perfect, but this car is one of the best. It's big and sturdy, and the occupants are surround by lots of steel. More than that, it has all of the safety features you want, like antilock brakes, a seatbelt lockout so she can't drive it unless everyone in the car is buckled...stuff like that.*

> *Nothing will make her 100% safe, but she won't be safer in any other vehicle than this. And it comes in red, too.*

Understanding his motivation allows us to tailor our message so it resonates with him, so it's relevant to him. It allows us to make our message more targeted and much more personal. This is far more effective than writing a generic statement that addresses the objective but not the underlying motivation.

A fictional story based on a real-life example

A buyer is looking for a payroll vendor that has the capability to receive and then process payroll information derived from a variety of sources such as time clocks, spreadsheets, automated time and attendance systems, etc. This is a clearly stated requirement and, all things considered, a pretty good place to start. A proposal writer could write some content in response to this need. But what's the motivation behind the requirement? Is there something more?

Suppose we discover that today, their current payroll vendor requires them to *manually* input employee hours into an online payroll submission system. This means that each office has to collect employee hours in whatever format they use at that office, and then manually input those hours into the online system. All this manual data entry is a process ripe for errors.

Then we learn the controller, Julie, is personally responsible for fixing all of the errors that happen through this manual input system. Julie, alone, has to reconcile all of the submissions. Julie, alone, has to fix all of the errors she finds. Worst of all, Julie, alone, has the unenviable job of retracting erroneous overpayments from employees *after checks are sent.* This whole effort is time consuming and tedious, and because she's retracting pay from people, it gives her a bad reputation in the company. Julie is unhappy.

Though sad for Julie, this is exactly the kind of back story that proposal writers dream about.

Let's fast forward. Julie issues an RFP, and one of the questions is this:

> *Describe your company's capability to receive and then process payroll information derived from a variety of sources.*

Without knowing the back story, some proposal writers would respond to this requirement using fairly stock content that says something like this:

> *We have the ability to accept employee payroll data in a variety of formats. You can enter it manually through our online data entry module, or you can submit payroll data electronically from many of the most popular accounting programs or time clock systems. If we don't currently offer support for your submission preference, we will work with you during implementation to design and build an interface that works for you.*

Clearly, this answer is compliant with the buyer's requirement; they want you to support their need to import their payroll data, and you acknowledge you do. You even pledge to implement something new if you don't provide it today. Good for you.

If you understood the backstory, though, if you understood the effort Julie invests each pay period and the anguish she feels at having to complete her regular reconciliation effort, you might change how you construct your response.

When organizations are required to submit payroll hours manually, there are inevitably lots of mistakes. Not only does someone in your organization have to reconcile all of your payroll records to find those mistakes, someone has to reach out to the employees who were affected to explain the errors and, in some cases, to recover the overpayments they received. Admitting payroll errors is not fun. Recovering overpayments you made is one job nobody wants.

We understand you submit payroll data differently depending on the office submitting it:

- *Five offices submit payroll data using Dave's Timeclock format.*

- *Three offices submit payroll data using Jane's Timeclock format.*

- *Thirteen of your offices, including your headquarters, submit payroll data electronically in the Amalgamated fictional ERP program format.*

- *Two remote offices submit payroll data manually.*

The solution we are proposing accommodates each of these formats. It will import data in Dave's Timeclock format, in Jane's Timeclock format, and in the format generated by your Amalgamated Fictional ERP system. This means no one will have to re-enter payroll data before submitting it to you for your review and approval.

We also make it as easy as possible for your two remote offices who currently submit payroll information manually. We've created a simple, online, user interface where payroll information can be entered. Before we process the file, though, we forward a confirmation copy of the payroll data back to your team. The confirmation copy highlights any pay data that is outside the historical range for that employee. This enables your staff to, in effect, research potential data entry errors before the payroll file is processed.

Between these measures, you can be confident that the number of payroll errors you experience, and the time to find and fix mistakes, is minimized.

This answer is longer, to be sure, but it's far more effective. To Julie, especially, this answer will be compelling. It means she won't have to spend nearly the time researching and fixing errors. Best of all, she won't be the bad guy anymore because she will no longer have to take back money that had been erroneously paid to an employee. This makes Julie happy.

Sell to people, not to organizations.

PERSONAL MOTIVATIONS VS. ORGANIZATIONAL OBJECTIVES

As we delve further into this discussion, it's important to recognize how personal motivations translate into corporate objectives. The following table describes personal motivations I've encountered over the years, and how those motivations were ultimately expressed in an RFP.

The buyers personal motivation	How the motivation was expressed in the RFP
My wife and I have hit a rough spot. I need to spend more time at home, and less time managing a great big, never-ending implementation.	The winning bidder will propose a solution that must be fully implemented within three business days during normal business hours.
I'm three years away from retirement and a sweet pension. There's no way I'm going out on a limb for something unproven, no matter what the potential upside is.	Extra points will be awarded to the bidder who presents a proven, mature application that is shown, through multiple implementations, to be reliable and dependable.

The last time I picked a vendor without buy-in from my user community, I heard about it for the next three months. They have to approve it, too.	User satisfaction is critical. The winning bidder must propose a program that is easy to use by all stakeholders within our user community.

It's important to recognize that, while organizational objectives can be so general that they could almost be cut and pasted across many different RFPs from as many buyers, every motivation is unique to a person. Understand the motive and you will have a much better understanding about the RFP verbiage it morphs into.

SOME MOTIVATIONS DON'T BECOME ORGANIZATIONAL OBJECTIVES

While many personal motivations are transformed into organizational objectives that eventually appear in RFPs, some never make it that far. For example, I was working once with a young manager who had great aspirations and was eager to move up in his organization. More than anything, he wanted recognition. More than anything, I wanted to make a sale.

One of my more experienced associates came up with the brilliant idea to write a case study showcasing this young manager and his plans to use our product to transform productivity within his department. We even put his picture on the front of the document, making it look like an article you might find in a trade magazine. This gave us another case study we could use, but more important, it gave him the exposure he wanted. We sent him a stack of the glossy documents, and he enthusiastically shared them around the office. He got the recognition he wanted and we made a sale.

The point of this story is motivations are personal and don't always translate into an RFP objective, but they are no less important. If you understand a person's personal motivation, and you can somehow address it, you are able to give them what they really want even though no other vendor responding to the RFP knows it's an issue.

HOW DO YOU LEARN WHAT EACH DECISION MAKER'S MOTIVATIONS ARE?

How do you discover their motivations? This question is, at the same time, one of the easiest questions to answer and one of the most difficult selling tasks you face.

If you want to learn what the decision maker's motivations are, you need to build a relationship with the decision maker. You need to get to know him or her personally. This doesn't happen overnight. Indeed, it doesn't happen unless you've developed a relationship with them and, over time, they come to trust you.

In the first example in the preceding table, the man shared something with me that was deeply personal—that he and his wife were having difficulties in their relationship. He never would have shared that if he hadn't known me, if we weren't already friends, and if he hadn't trusted me.

The point is you can't just swoop in and expect someone to share their personal thoughts and feelings and motivations with you. Building a relationship takes time. And this goes back to the very first best practice presented in this book—*you have to be proactive.*

If you want to write customer-focused proposals, if you want to understand the buyer's true motivations, you have to start calling on accounts in the 24 months before the RFP comes out. Only then will you have the time needed to gain someone's confidence and truly understand what they truly care about. You have to invest the time.

A PERCEPTION OF RISK IS ONE OF THE MOST POWERFUL MOTIVATORS

Speaking of motivations, I'd be derelict if I didn't mention one of the most powerful motivators of all—*risk.*

Nothing will kill a sale faster than if a buyer perceives too much risk. Notice I use the word, *perceive.* Risk is not a fact, it's a perception, and different people have different perceptions. This necessarily means that in any given interaction with a buyer, it's not what you know to be true, the only thing that matters is what they perceive to be true.

You are invited to present to a potential new client. You're in the conference room with the two buyers making the all-important coffee cup buying decision. "We're one of the largest providers of branded coffee cups in the region," you exclaim with pride.

- **Buyer 1 perception**: *Oh, that's good. They must have the resources and infrastructure to support our business.*
- **Buyer 2 perception**: *Oh, no, they're much too big for our small business. There's no chance we're going to get the same kind of attention as their larger customers.*

Which of these perceptions is true? The answer is both are true because each perception is true to the person who believes it. This is one of the things that makes selling so challenging; there are rarely absolutes. Something you perceive to be a benefit may be viewed by someone else as a liability. Something you perceive to be a liability may be viewed by someone else as a benefit.

Sometimes, you may encounter a generalized sense of risk shared among most or all of the decision makers. Suppose the last two companies they hired went out of business before the contract was completed. On the next procurement, therefore, they're likely going to try to minimize that "risk" by hiring a company that's been in business longer, is larger, has solid financial statements, etc.

More often, a perception of risk is personal. For example, Dan in accounting has worked with smaller vendors who don't always have great quality processes in their invoicing systems. These vendors require a lot more involvement from him because he has to double check and reconcile everything they send. The larger companies he has worked with generally have more sophisticated systems and produce invoices that are consistently accurate. So, while little ABC Fictional Coffee Cup Company might provide a good product at a competitive price, Dan harbors a sense of risk that their invoicing systems are below par.

> Nothing else you say is relevant if the buyer perceives your product, solution, or company as being too risky.

This is why it's so important for your salespeople and business development people to be proactive, to meet and get to know all of the buyers involved in the procurement long before the RFP comes out. If you can figure out what their motivations are, and especially their perceptions of risk, you'll be in a much better position to address them and give your company a legitimate shot at winning the business.

CHAPTER RECAP

Organizations don't buy things, people do. So while the requirements they list in their RFPs are important, and we have to address them in our proposals, recognize that those requirements are driven by personal motivations. Said another way, it was someone's personal motivation—an issue, a concern, an interest—that ultimately became an organizational requirement. If you understand the personal motivation, you have the keys to making a sale.

Sell to people, not to organizations.

6. Differentiate Your Solution

From a buyers' perspective—*and it does not matter what industry you are in*—a vendor is a vendor is a vendor. From their perspective, you are all the same. You act the same, describe your products or services the same, deliver the same kind of service, and probably even offer the same level of service. Whether you sell office copiers, audit services, enterprise accounting tools, departmental servers, banking services, landscaping services, janitorial services, leased fleet vehicles—*whatever you sell*—you're all the same! You're identical! YOU'RE A COMMODITY!

It's those last three words that are particularly terrible to hear, the single worst accusation most business professionals will ever encounter. It's terrible because when you're a commodity, nobody cares about value. Nobody cares about the quality of work you do. All that matters is who has the lowest price.

"But wait a minute," you protest, in a rather defensive voice, "we are not a commodity! We employ some of the best people in our field. We've had more innovations last year than our two major competitors combined. Our customer service program is recognized in the industry and regularly gets awards. We are NOT a commodity, we are unique, we are different, we are better!"

I would expect you to respond this way. In fact, I've never met a business development person (worth his or her salt) who thought they were selling a commodity product or service, and to a person, they bristle against being labeled that way.

But then I push back against their argument: "OK, I believe you, you are not a commodity. There are things you do that are different and better than what your competitors do. But here's the key question you need to ask: *does that message come across clearly in your proposals?"*

This is the all-important question, and it should give business development people—from managers to salespeople to proposal writers—reason to pause and ponder. Seriously pause. Seriously ponder.

Here is an exercise you might find enlightening.

- Read a section of a proposal you recently wrote. Now ask yourself, except for identifiable stuff like your name, if you copied this entire section, could you paste it into a competitor's proposal as is? Would it be just as true in their proposal as it is in yours?

- Next, read a section of one of your competitor's proposals they recently wrote. Now ask yourself, except for identifiable stuff like their name, if you copied the entire section, could you paste it into your proposal as is? Would it be just as true in your proposal as it is in theirs?

As you work through this exercise, be honest with yourself. Remember, it's just an exercise.

Sure, some sections will necessarily be uniquely focused on you. But I'd wager some sections and maybe even most sections will be so generic they could apply equally to your company or your competition.

When this happens, you aren't differentiating your business or your solution. To the contrary; if your content is this generic, you are inadvertently providing evidence that you are, in fact, generically similar—*a commodity*. When this happens, the buyer is asking herself, "Why should I buy from Company A when I can get the same service from Company B for less money?

Buyers want to make good decisions

The reality is most buyers want to make good purchase decisions. They aren't necessarily looking for just the lowest price, most are honestly and sincerely looking for the best overall solution and value for their organizations. But here's the problem.

Your buyers are not experts in your industry like you are. They don't understand all the differences between the office copier you sell and the office copiers that your competitors sell. Indeed, when faced with a myriad array of office copier alternatives, they're unsure and uncertain, and probably even a bit confused.

They know they want to reduce overall costs, for example, but they may not know the operating costs of your office copier are half of your competitors' copiers' operating cost. They don't know that while your copier is more expensive initially, it will save them thousands of dollars over its operational life. All they know is the initial price tag of your copier is $500 more than your competitor's copier—*and that is a differentiator.*

In the same position, which copier would you choose? Lacking a better understanding, you'd probably go with the less expensive copier. After all, why pay more than you have to if you believe all the copiers are the same? And unless someone educates you otherwise, from your perspective, all the copiers are all the same.

The point bears repeating: most buyers want to make good purchase decisions and get the best value for their organizations, but they don't always know how to make the best decision. They don't always have the information they need to be able to differentiate between the various vendors and options that are available. We assume they know, but often as not, they don't. They need someone to educate them about the differences so they can make informed decisions. That someone is you.

WHY SHOULD I BUY FROM YOU?

When you are writing proposals in response to RFPs, it's not enough to show you comply with their requirements. It's not enough to demonstrate you meet their minimum qualifications. It is on you to answer a question, the all-important question, even when the buyer isn't overt or explicit in asking it themselves: *"Why should I buy from you?"*

- Do you offer us something the others don't?
- Is your service faster or more efficient?
- Is your program easier to implement?

- Does your product return greater dividends? Lower long-term costs?
- Are your offices closer to ours than those of other vendors?
- Is your company more financially stable in this current period of economic uncertainty?

The buyer wants to know the answers to these questions. Your challenge is to articulate why your solution is both *different* and *better* than the solutions your competitors are offering and, ultimately, to give them an answer to, *"Why should I buy from you?"*

THE COMMON PRACTICE = BE TIMID

When I teach proposal writing classes and we begin discussing differentiators, someone almost always says something like, "we do a pretty good job with that." When we start reviewing their proposal content, though, it always strikes me how timid writers can be when articulating their competitive strengths.

Sometimes, proposal writers are hesitant to articulate differentiators because they don't want to seem too pushy, or they don't want to appear too negative towards the competition. Other times, they aren't entirely confident their internal legal departments will let them make big claims. Still other times, it's almost as if they lack someone standing behind them, encouraging them to push a bit further. Whatever the reason, when we fail to communicate why our solution is preferable to anyone else's, we're doing a disservice to ourselves and to our customers.

- We're doing a disservice to ourselves because if we don't tell them why we're different and better, who will? We're allowing ourselves to be dismissed as a commodity vendor with no unique value to offer.
- We're doing a disservice to our customers because, as we've discussed, they want to make good decisions, and by extension, to understand what makes us different and better than the competition. If we don't tell them, they won't know.

If you want to improve the quality of your proposals, you must find a way to articulate your differences and your strengths more boldly.

THE BEST PRACTICE = BOLDLY SAY WHY YOU'RE DIFFERENT AND BETTER!

When communicating differentiators, you can't just hint at your differences and strengths. You can't just reference them in some passing way, or bury them in text somewhere deep within your proposal and then hope the buyer will read it and understand its significance.

You have to be explicit, even forceful. You must find a way to say—clearly, boldly, and without ambiguity—why the solution you are proposing is both different and better than any other solution the buyer may be considering.

> *Mr. Customer, there are ten different companies that sell an office copier that will meet your needs. But here are three compelling reasons why our copier is a better fit for your needs than any other copier solution you may be considering...*

Figure out how to effectively differentiate your solution from competing solutions, figure out how to articulate your unique competitive advantage, and you will never again be labeled or considered a commodity.

TWO COMPONENTS OF A GOOD DIFFERENTIATOR

Differentiators must incorporate two things to be effective; they must be customer-focused, and they must explain not just why your solution is different but also why it's better.

It has to be customer-focused

To be effective, a differentiator must be focused on the unique needs of a specific buyer. Suppose your company just won an award for having one of the most comprehensive distribution networks in the region. This is great news for your company. You deserve accolades. But suppose the buyer you're working with today is a small mom and pop shop primarily interested in finding a vendor with awesome local support. You can talk about your award-winning distribution network all you want, but it will likely fall on deaf ears. It's a differentiator, to be sure, but it's not relevant to this buyer.

Differentiators only work if they're aligned with a customer need, concern, or interest. If you are selling to a woman-owned business, and you just won industry recognition for your commitment to promoting women in the workplace, emphasize it. If you are selling to an organization that is geographically diverse, and you have multiple offices located in close proximity to theirs, highlight it. If your business is focused on a particular region, but your competitors are all national organizations focused on everywhere, emphasize your focus on and commitment to the local community. Don't focus on *value* if they are focused on *low cost*, and don't focus on *low cost* if they are focused on *value*.

To be effective, *your differentiators must align with their interests.*

It's not enough to be different

Today, the business community uses words like "business strengths" and "differentiators." I use these words also because people today understand what they mean. When I went to school in the 80's, though, I was taught to use a different term, and it's one that I still prefer: *unique competitive advantage.* I like this old-fashioned term because it recognizes it's not enough to be different, you must also be better.

If your competitor paints their office copier red, and you paint yours blue, that's certainly a differentiator. But just because it's different doesn't make it better. The whole idea of *unique competitive advantage* is you are selling something that is different and, in some way, also better for the buyer. It provides an advantage over what your competitors are able to provide. Consider this example.

> *Unlike most of our competitors who only offer red copiers, we also offer blue copiers that coordinate well with your silver and blue corporate color scheme. Not only does our copier provide the performance you expect, it will look like it's custom-made for your office.*

A cheesy example, perhaps, but you get the idea—it can't just be different, it has to be better.

Ghosting the competition

"Ghosting" is proposal industry jargon. It's a term proposal professionals employ when they're working to position their solutions against competitive alternatives.

For our purposes here, ghosting refers to highlighting a competitor's weaknesses—and your strengths—without referencing the competitor by name.

> *Unlike some coffee cup manufacturers who are struggling financially in today's difficult economy, and a few who are working through bankruptcy reorganization, we remain both profitable and debt-free.*

Make certain the weakness you highlight is genuine. The example above is a good one—*provided* you are financially strong in an economy where others are struggling. However, embellishing the truth to your advantage, or even making up differences where none exist, demonstrate a lack of integrity and undermine your credibility. Don't do it.

Some countries have rules about competitive claims

I was teaching a class to a company here in the U.S., and some of their associates were dialed in from Europe. When we started talking about differentiators, they quickly educated me about what they are and are not allowed to say in their promotional materials.

Essentially, they told me that in Europe, you can talk about your strengths but you cannot talk about your competitors' weaknesses. That is viewed negatively and could open you up to legal challenges.

The previous example about financial strength would not be acceptable because it mentions competitors' weaknesses. However, it could be reworded to emphasize their strengths without drawing a contrast to others' weaknesses:

> *Today's economy is challenging for all vendors. One of the things that makes us unique is that despite this difficult economy, we remain both profitable and debt free.*

Differentiation can be difficult if you aren't allowed to call out your competitors' weaknesses; nevertheless, do not miss an opportunity to highlight your strengths.

HOW TO WRITE DIFFERENTIATORS IN YOUR PROPOSALS

The way you present your differentiators and strengths may change depending on where they appear in your proposal.

Answering RFP questions

If you are drafting an answer to an RFP question, and it's an area where you have a unique competitive advantage, then be sure to highlight your advantage in your response.

Q. How many offices do you have currently?

A. We currently have 22 offices spread across Ohio, Michigan, and Indiana. It's also worth noting that we have an office within 10 miles of each of your offices.

This is an important distinction.

Unlike many coffee cup vendors that are more nationally-focused, our regional focus and close proximity means each of your offices will receive better and more focused attention than a national vendor could ever hope to provide.

In this example, we answer their question, but we also take the opportunity to explain why our offering is both different from what others offer and better for this particular buyer.

Differentiators are ribbons that weave throughout your proposal

When you're writing a proposal, you don't want to limit your discussion of differentiators to one section or one answer, you should include them throughout your proposal in appropriate places where they are most relevant. Remember, our goal is not just to be compliant, we aren't just answering a questionnaire, our singular purpose is to make a sale.

Therefore, whenever you're answering a question, ask yourself if it makes sense to include verbiage that transforms your answer into a differentiator.

Answering a question dedicated to differentiators

Many RFPs include a question specifically asking what differences you offer versus your competitors. In these cases, I recommend structuring your answer with this four step approach:

1. Use a bold heading for each differentiator you list
2. Acknowledge the issue or challenge that is facing the buyer.
3. Use a statement that clearly indicates that your solution offers a better alternative.
4. Explain how your solution is better.
5. Explain what it means to them.

It's important to note that this structure is more like a starting point; how you ultimately write your differentiator will vary based on many factors. In the examples that follow, I sometimes switch steps 3 and 4, or I blend steps 4 and 5. That's OK.

Be bold by contrasting your solution from others

The important point about writing differentiators is you cannot be meek. There can be no ambiguity. You have to be bold and clear in your telling. The reader must understand that your solution is different and better than what other vendors are offering. One of the best ways to accomplish this is to boldly contrast your solution with theirs.

My preferred approach is to include a paragraph that reiterates what you understand the client wants. Then, I begin the second paragraph with verbiage that highlights the contrast:

- *Unlike other vendors that…*
- *While other vendors do it that way, we're different.*
- *We take a different approach.*
- *What sets us apart from these other vendors is…*

Sometimes, I even put this transition statement in between two paragraphs, a paragraph of its own so it stands out more clearly. I've found this technique to be extremely effective. As you review the following examples, be sure to notice the use of contrast to articulate what makes us different from other vendors.

DIFFERENTIATOR EXAMPLES

Following are some examples that are completely made up but based on the reality of past experience. Remember, each of these would be written in your proposal based on the need of a particular client. With a few tweaks, the actual content could be included in answers to questions, in the executive introduction, in customer references, etc.

We have the infrastructure to support your operations

Buyer is a large company with offices throughout the United States and Canada. You want an office copier supply house that has a geographic service area large enough to service your offices across your entire operational area. At Dave's Fictional Office Copier Supply Company, we do.

Unlike many of our competitors that are regional or local, Dave's is an international organization with offices in major cities throughout the US and Canada. This means we are able to provide local service to each of your offices, regardless of location. While smaller providers are trying to provide service from other cities or even other countries, our professional staff is onsite providing your staff with more focused attention and personal service.

We're right-sized to provide you the service you expect

One of the problems being a small business buying from a large vendor is you don't always get the attention you need. That's because larger vendors tend to focus most of their attention on their larger customers that generate larger revenue.

At Dave's Fictional Office Copier Supply Company, we're different.

Dave's is a local small business, and just like you, we've built our business providing high-quality sales and service to other small businesses throughout the tristate area. We still have all of the resources you'd expect from a full service vendor—qualified service staff, expansive inventory, an impressive parts warehouse—but we provide all of these things with the kind of focused, "we know your first name" service that our local clientele has come to expect.

Twenty-four hour service = no downtime

You rely on your copier, so if it should ever need service, you want to know that you can get it fixed without having to wait a day or more for a service technician.

Unlike other copier vendors that only offer support services during normal business hours, we offer you access to our service technicians seven days a week, twenty-four hours a day. If you ever have a problem, there's always someone you can call for help. This means you will never be stuck in a situation where you can't get the help you need.

Emergency Replacement

Copiers are complex machines. And while our line of copiers has one of the best reliability ratings in the industry, it is unrealistic to suggest that one of our copiers will never break. So at Dave's Fictional Office Copier Supply Company, we formulated a contingency plan for our customers, like you, who rely on your copier as a normal and routine part of your operations.

If your copier is ever out of order for more than twenty-four hours, we will provide you with an emergency replacement until we can repair your copier to full operational status. This exceptional level of service is uncommon in our industry, but it's all part of the service commitment we make to our customers.

Access to the owner means more responsive service

At Dave's Fictional Office Copier Supply Company, we make a promise to each and every customer that you will receive the very best service possible. These are more than just words; this is the fundamental principle around which we've built our organization.

We are so confident in the quality service we deliver that we provide each customer with the name and direct phone number of the president and owner of our firm. If you are ever not satisfied with the service you receive, you have access to the person who can make it right.

Will any of the large, national vendors give you the personal phone number of the owner?

Experienced instructor

Some organizations hire professional trainers to deliver their proposal training programs. While these professional presenters are typically very polished they are not necessarily experienced in writing proposals in response to RFPs. They've never been in the trenches. They lack depth.

We take a different approach.

The person who will be teaching the class we are proposing is Paul Writer. Paul has been writing and managing proposal projects for more than 20 years. This is an important distinction. If a student has a question, chances are Paul has experienced the same thing before, recalls how they addressed it, and can offer considered commentary based on his experience. You can be confident the instructor who teaches your class will have the depth of experience to offer an insightful, content-rich program that will help your staff to develop and grow professionally, and win more business.

When writing differentiators, be bold. Be brave. Be clear. Have the confidence in the solution you're selling to say, with heart, "we are the best solution for your organization and here's why..." Your customers will appreciate your candor.

CHAPTER RECAP

When writing a proposal, when differentiating your solution from the competition, don't be shy. You must find a way to say—clearly, boldly, and without ambiguity—why the solution you are proposing is different and better than any other solution the buyer may be considering.

7. Make Your Proposals Easy to Skim (and Score)

Nobody reads a proposal cover to cover. Period.

This tidbit of insight should not come as a shock to any businessperson, though. That's because anyone who has been in business for any length of time knows businesspeople are busy. In fact, the word *business* comes from the Middle English *bisynesse*; bisy (means you're busy), and nesse (the state of being busy). When you translate *bisynesse* into modern English, it means "people who are too busy to read a lengthy proposal."

In the proposal seminars I teach, I ask students, "Do any of you have time in your day to read a 75-page proposal *cover to cover*?" Some say, "no," some just shake their heads in resignation at the blatant futility of writing long proposals that no one reads, and a few just sigh in surrender. But no one, not a single person, in all my years of training and proposal seminars, has ever said they have time to stop everything they are doing to read an entire 75-page proposal cover to cover.

After giving the class sufficient time to digest that question, I challenge them with another: "Now put yourself in the position of the buyer—businesspeople just like yourselves, people who have busy schedules just like yours, who have regular jobs and responsibilities in addition to reviewing proposals, and answer this question: do you have time in your day to read and carefully evaluate not one but five or six 75-page proposals from as many vendors?" "No," they each conclude, no one has sufficient time to read and carefully evaluate five or six 75-page proposals cover-to-cover. So the conclusion is—are you ready for this?— *no one reads your proposal cover to cover.*

No one reads your proposal cover to cover

This is hard for many sellers to accept. We spend lots of time pulling together proposals, deciding on graphics, stressing over messaging, and fretting over word choice. So when we are faced with the stark reality that no one is reading all that we write, many feel deflated. Almost dejected.

The good news is there's no reason to feel deflated or dejected because, candidly, it doesn't matter if they don't read your proposal cover to cover. The only thing that matters is if the document you send is able to influence their decision in your favor.

"OK," you may say, "but how can we influence their decision if they don't even read the proposal?" Good question!

Best practice—write for skimmers, not readers

The happiest and most successful people in this world are those who can look at a situation and see it as it is, not as they wish it to be. Accepting this, our job as proposal writers is to do everything we can to make our proposals easy to skim. We need to construct our proposals so the decision maker can comprehend what we're proposing—including why it benefits her and why the solution we are offering is better than what anyone else is proposing—even if she only has 20 or 30 minutes to review the document.

> The reality is while most will not read your entire proposal, almost everyone will at least read some parts of your proposal, but only after skimming it to find the parts that interest them.

Therefore, the challenge before us is to construct our proposals to make them easy for the reader to skim quickly, understand the larger message we're trying to communicate, and then find the sections they want to read in more depth.

Making your proposals easy to skim

If you design your proposals so they are easy to skim, not just easy to read, you're going to be far more effective at communicating your message to, and hopefully persuading, those busy decision makers who lack the time to read the entire proposal.

Listed here are six things you can do to make your proposals easier to skim.

1. USE LOTS OF HEADINGS AND SUBHEADINGS

Of all the things you can do to make your proposals easier to skim, the easiest and most effective is to use lots of headings and subheadings throughout the body of your document.

Suppose you're one of those "bisynesse" people we talked about who does not have time to read a proposal cover to cover. Suppose you open a proposal to a section that interests you and you're confronted with an uninterrupted block of text a page long. "Arghhh," you mutter under your breath. It's discouraging. It's disheartening. It's dispiriting. Heck, it's even deflating. So you skip it.

Now suppose you look at that same page, but it's been edited to include headings and subheadings that organize all that text into logical ideas, groups, or concepts. You don't have to read the entire thing to understand it, all you have to do is browse quickly through the headings and subheadings until you comprehend the message they're trying to share and find the information you want.

Consider how this chapter is organized around headings and subheadings. After the chapter title, it's organized into three headings with seven subheadings. If I compile these into an abstract, it looks like this:

- ❖ No one reads your proposal cover to cover
- ❖ Write for skimmers, not readers
- ❖ Making your proposals easy to skim
  - ➢ Use lots of headings and subheadings
  - ➢ Provide a summary answer prior to your complete answer

- ➤ Introduce each new 'chapter' or major section with a mini executive introduction
- ➤ Use callout boxes for mini case studies
- ➤ Use callout boxes for quotes
- ➤ Use charts, graphs, and pictures

If someone is busy, if she doesn't have time to read every word, she can still understand the fundamental message by reading only these headings and subheadings. This approach is important in any kind of business writing, but it's especially important in a sales document, and most especially in a proposal.

Here's a short exercise. Find a recent proposal you wrote and find a page or a couple pages of uninterrupted text. Now take five or ten minutes to find logical places to add some headings. Be careful in your wording. Remember our goal is for the reader to understand our message if all they do is read the headings and subheadings. Hopefully, you'll find it's not that difficult to do, but you'll also find it makes your proposals a lot easier to read.

There are many things you can do to make your proposal easier to skim, but headings and subheadings are one of the easiest and most effective.

2. PROVIDE A SUMMARY ANSWER PRIOR TO YOUR COMPLETE ANSWER

For many buying organizations—especially state and local governments and school districts—evaluating your proposal means reviewing and scoring each of your answers. That's a fairly simple and straightforward statement, but let's pause for a moment and consider what this means from the perspective of the reviewer.

People who are drafted onto a review committee generally aren't just sitting around waiting for a proposal review project to come their way. They have other jobs and other responsibilities, and the proposal review project they've just been assigned is in addition to their existing workload. So what does this mean to us?

From the seller's perspective, it means our proposal is being reviewed by someone who likely doesn't have sufficient time to review it, who isn't motivated to review it carefully, and likely, who is inclined to take shortcuts based more on temporal expediency than meticulous and painstaking consideration. In other words, you're relying on someone whose attitude is, "I hope I do a good job, but it's really not that important to me, so I want to get it off my plate as quickly as possible."

As sellers, we must understand that this is often the context in which we are working. It may not be ideal, but it is what it is. We have to accept it as it is, we have to embrace it as it is, and if we're going to benefit from it, we have to develop a strategy to address it.

With all of this as a background, our path becomes clear; we need to find a way to make it as easy as possible for the reader to determine whether the answers we present are compliant at a minimum, and ideally, provide some additional benefit. Thankfully, this isn't too difficult.

Include summary answers

A summary answer is a short paragraph that you include immediately following their question and immediately preceding your answer. In addition to demonstrating compliance, if possible, its purpose is to summarize your answer in one or two sentences.

To make it as easy as possible for the reader, your answer summary should be set apart with some unique formatting and perhaps a unique graphic.

Here are a few examples of different summary answers you might consider including if you're selling Fictional brand office copiers.

 Fully compliant. The office copier we are proposing is accessible from your network, and fully compliant with the specifications documented in your question.

 Partially compliant. The office copier we are proposing is partially compliant with your requirements. It will work with your existing network, but it's not plug-n-play as you request, it must be manually configured.

Will be compliant. The office copier we are proposing is not currently compliant, but it will be by your targeted implementation date. The networking feature is completed and is currently in the final testing phase.

Not compliant. The office copier we are proposing does not support networking.

Alternative solution. The office copier we are proposing does support networking, but it uses an alternative approach from what is mandated in your specifications. Our answer explains why we believe our approach is more beneficial for your needs.

I like using the compliance headings—"Fully Compliant," "Partially compliant," etc.—where possible and when it makes sense. It makes it easier for reviewers to determine compliance with program requirements without having to do a lot of work figuring it out on their own.

If you use this approach, though, it's important to be honest when writing each summary. It undermines your credibility if you say you are compliant when you're not; they won't believe anything else you say. If you're compliant, say it. If you aren't, admit it.

Not all answer summaries are compliance statements, they're just summaries

Some questions don't specifically ask compliance-related questions. For example, suppose the question is stated like this, "Please describe your customer service program," or "Please describe your quality program and how it will benefit Buyer."

These are more like essay questions rather than yes or no compliance questions, so you can't answer the same way. Still, I prefer to use the answer summary technique, but I exclude the compliance heading. Here are a couple examples:

Q. Please describe your quality program and how it will benefit buyer.

 Seller has a sophisticated quality program that is fully documented, codified, and managed by Dan Jones, our VP of Product Quality. The following answer details the program Dan put in place to ensure consistent quality standards are met.

Q. Please describe your customer service program and how it benefits buyer.

 Our customer service program is built on responsiveness and transparency. The following description, which includes customer testimonials, offers proof into its effectiveness.

Preceding each of your proposal answers with a summary answer is a relatively simple approach, but it's also highly effective. It's effective because you're making it incredibly easy for the reviewer to quickly evaluate your answer, and quickly complete their review of your proposal. For someone who doesn't have a lot of time, and whose commitment to the project is teetering on the brink of "*I don't care,*" your summary is going to be well-received, and that is going to reflect positively on you when they assign points.

Answer summary length

Answer summaries should never be more than a sentence or two, or longer than three or four lines. To be clear, an answer summary is where you provide a concise answer, not where you prove the claim. Immediately following the answer summary—in the answer you provide—is where you include your complete answer and evidence.

Advantages of using answer summaries

There's another advantage to using answer summaries and it's got to do with one of our other goals—communicating persuasively. Whenever someone is presented with new information, it takes effort to evaluate the information, its significance, and what it means to them. It doesn't sound like it's much work but, in fact, this kind of cerebral reasoning is a relatively strenuous mental exercise.

There's a huge difference between making an assessment yourself and evaluating someone else's assessment. By including an answer summary at the beginning of each answer, you're doing all the hard work, all the heavy lifting, because you're making the assessment for them. All the reviewer has to do is decide whether he agrees with your assessment. This makes it much easier for him or her to make a conclusion.

Since I started using this approach years ago, I've received a lot of positive response, not just from my customers but also from their customers, the people who review proposals. They like it because it makes their jobs easier.

3. INTRODUCE EACH NEW 'CHAPTER' OR MAJOR SECTION WITH A MINI EXECUTIVE INTRODUCTION

Another effective technique to make it easier for readers to skim your proposal is to draft a short introduction at the beginning of each major section. Notice I say *introduction*, not *summary*. It's an important distinction.

A summary is just that; it attempts to summarize into a few concise paragraphs everything that was written in that section. The problem is a section with 10 or 20 disparate questions doesn't lend itself well to being summarized.

Instead of summarizing, therefore, I prefer to *introduce* the section by telling the reader what he will learn when he reads it. These introductions should be short—three or four paragraphs—and they should be formatted so they are distinct from the rest of the text. Further and perhaps most to the point, they should highlight the major points of your message, the key takeaways, the things you want the buyer to remember as she reviews the section.

An example of a section introduction

Suppose the buyer includes a section in their RFP asking about your quality program, and more specifically, what systems or processes you use to consistently deliver a quality product or service. An introduction to that section might read something like this:

In your RFP, you make clear that a vendor's ability to deliver consistent service quality is one of your primary objectives. We provide quality service, consistently, and in this section we demonstrate how.

In this section, you will learn four important things:

- *We built an internal quality department where auditors, independent of each department, reconcile actual performance against expectations and established procedures.*

- *We created a senior management position to oversee this department, to intervene when a quality measure falls below an established threshold, and to report findings to management.*

- *We report all of our quality findings to each client, making you aware of our actual performance.*

- *We back up our quality approach with service level agreements, SLAs, in which we are penalized if we do not meet agreed performance standards.*

You can be confident we will deliver the consistent quality you seek. In the rest of this section, we answer each of your questions and explain, in greater detail, exactly how we deliver the quality levels we promise.

If we think about those poor reviewers who don't have enough time to read every word of every proposal they're tasked with reviewing, but are nevertheless required to complete those reviews while still completing their other assigned work, this introduction is wonderful! It gives them a way to quickly skim our proposal document while still getting the essence of the solution we're proposing and what it means to them, but do it in a fraction of the time it would otherwise involve.

It's also persuasive

There's another, secondary benefit we gain from this approach. If you tell the reviewer what they're going to learn, beforehand, you've framed the conversation. You've prepared them to be looking for certain things, the important things, they need to learn and take away from all of the information you present. This is itself persuasive and here's why.

When faced with reviewing a document, a reader has to evaluate everything he reads and then process, organize, and evaluate the information. What does it mean? How does it impact me? Is this good for me or problematic? This process takes time and mental effort for the reader to complete. If you can help him by sharing, beforehand, what he should be looking for, by explaining what the information means to him, he's going to be better able to process the information more easily when he sees it.

4. USE CALLOUT BOXES FOR MINI CASE STUDIES

In a previous chapter, we discussed using mini case studies as evidence to support persuasive arguments. The other reason we like to use mini case studies is because short, two or three paragraph case studies, presented in callout boxes within the body of a proposal, are a great way to make it easy for a reviewer to skim your proposal quickly. If a picture is worth a thousand words, a well-written case study is worth a thousand pictures.

If I'm the superintendent of a small, rural school system, and I'm trying to choose a school admin software application for my district, I would likely be interested in the experiences of another small school system, like mine, who faced the same decision. I'd be interested in the approach they used, the thought processes they employed, and obviously, what they ultimately decided.

This is precisely why case studies can be so effective within the sales process; they summarize how others have approached and resolved the same decision the buyer is now facing. We call it a case study, but to the buyer, it's almost as if it's a short tutorial on how to approach the decision they're about to make.

If the case study stands out and is short enough it can be read in a couple minutes, reviewers will likely take a moment to pause their skimming and read what it has to say.

> ### How ABC School Software Helps Small, Rural Schools Get Big Results
>
> Like many rural schools, Small Fictional School District was limited on IT resources. This presented a problem when it came time to implement a new school administration system.
>
> After evaluating many alternatives, Small chose Dave's Fictional School Software. Since it's cloud based, the need for District IT resources was minimized. Also, because Dave's provided onsite support during implementation, the demands on the school's limited IT resources was minimized even more.
>
> "We couldn't be more pleased," said Sally Jones, superintendent. "The entire implementation process was so easy—it was almost a non-event. And everyone is thrilled with the capabilities of the new system. We looked at a lot of vendors, but Dave's was right-sized for us.

Writing a case study for a proposal

Case studies included within the body text of a proposal should incorporate two design components to improve its skimmability:

1. It should be included in a callout box located within the section being discussed. Callout boxes stand out and reviewers will read them even when they don't read everything else.
2. It should include a bold heading with a clear statement about the message you want to share. The reader should be able to tell, at a glance, how it relates to them.

The body of your case study should be no more than two or three paragraphs. The first paragraph should outline the problem. The second paragraph should document the solution. The third paragraph should describe the outcome the buyer received.

Clearly, it would be easy to add lots more information to your case study. It would be tempting, for example, to discuss all of the important features the buyer needed that only you could provide. Resist the temptation!

Remember that your goal is not to say everything, your goal is to make a case study that is easy to skim.

5. USE CALLOUT BOXES FOR QUOTES

Like mini case studies, including customer quotes in callout boxes is a great way to improve skimmability. They tell a story in a short space, and they're often compelling.

There really aren't that many rules when it comes to using quotes in your proposals, but there are a couple you must always abide by:

1. Make certain the quotes you use are relevant to the sections where they appear.
2. Keep your quotes short and to the point. Long, rambling quotes are nowhere near as effective.

Where quotes are particularly effective

Over many years of writing proposals, I've found that quotes can be particularly effective when discussing capabilities that are especially difficult to prove. Customer service is an excellent example.

Every vendor claims to have good customer service. In fact, I've never read proposal verbiage or heard a seller admit that their customer service was anything less than stellar. In the real world, though, most of us are immediately suspicious when a vendor starts talking about it because,

> *We couldn't be more pleased with ACME's customer service. When we had a question, they responded. When we had a problem, they fixed it. I only wish all vendors were this awesome.*

despite claims to the contrary, we've all encountered so many situations where customer service was decidedly less than stellar. The point is some things, like customer service, are very difficult to prove. This is the perfect context to pull out some good quotes.

A vendor can say, "we have great customer service," but most buyers would be justifiably suspicious. In contrast, an existing customer can say, "they have outstanding customer service," and it means so much more.

6. USE CHARTS, GRAPHS, AND PICTURES

People process information in different ways, but most—as many as 65% by some estimates—are visual learners; they prefer to process new information visually than read a lot of text. This is why many people find charts, graphs, and pictures to be far more compelling than pages and pages of text. It gives them a way to absorb the new information efficiently and quickly.

One of the big reasons I like visuals is because they can make it far easier for buyers to quickly skim a proposal and understand your message, even if they do not read every word in the section.

Use easy-to-understand charts

Charts are an excellent tool for proposal writers because they can communicate a lot of information at a glance.

But the challenge is to make your charts exceedingly simple to understand. This is important. I've seen some charts that were so complicated it would have been faster and easier to read an entire page of text than to figure out the chart's complexity. Complex charts don't help.

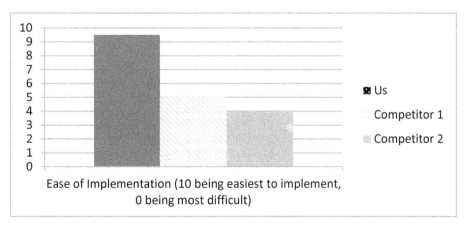

Simple-to-understand charts, in contrast, are totally awesome. Notice I don't say, "simple," just "simple-to-understand." The chart can have a hugely complex message just as long as someone can glance at it and understand it quickly without having to invest much brain power.

Suppose you know ease of installation is one of the buyer's primary buying criteria. In response, you engaged an independent agency to research how easy it is to implement services from the top three vendors. The results of that study showed, on a scale of 1 to 10, your program is by far the easiest to implement. This preceding graph—which is both simple *and* simple-to-understand—makes it clear that your program is easiest to implement. If the reader is interested in ease of implementation, then he or she can read your text to learn the data set on which your chart was created and the evidence to support the claim you make. Still, the claim is clear and easy-to-understand which makes it ideal for all of those reviewers who are skimming rather than reading your proposal.

About using color

Mass market business books like this one tend to use black and white rather than color, so most of the images in this book are in varying shades of gray. In proposals, though, sellers have more freedom to use color—and we tend to use it with reckless abandon. This is great, of course, *except* for your reviewers who are colorblind.

If you are using color artistically in an effort to make your proposals look pretty, this discussion doesn't really apply. Even colorblind people who only see a fraction of the range of colors you do appreciate your use of color.

Where the use of color matters most is when you use it to communicate information—as is common in many charts and graphs. For example, if you construct a pie chart that lists company divisions, and division one is the blue slice, division two is the purple slice, division three is the dark green slice, and division four is the brown slice, many of your colorblind readers may not easily understand the information you're trying to communicate. That's because the blue and purple may look very similar, and the dark green and brown might be, for many, indistinguishable. If you add in magenta or burgundy, forget about it—

they're all just varying shades of dark. In fact, if presented with the above pallet, I'd have to ask someone for help to understand which color is associated with each division. And then I'd have to take out a pen and write the name of each division on each pie slice.

This is why I generally suggest labeling each pie slice on the chart, or sticking to bold and distinct primary colors like dark blue, light blue, bright red, bright yellow, and Kelly green. If you need even more colors in your pallet, consider adding patterns to the brighter colors (yellow, light blue, and Kelly green). These simple steps will make your charts and graphs more universally understandable, even to people who only see a small fraction of the color pallet you do.

Last but not least, find someone on your staff who is red-green colorblind. The red-green version is most common, and it affects about 8% of men (only .5% of women) so you should be able to find someone without too much effort. Then, as a test, ask this person to evaluate your chart and see if he can correctly interpret the various colors in the chart's legend.

Using color is much like using jargon; it can be a very efficient way to communicate information, but only if everyone understands the jargon or sees the colors you're using. If they don't understand the jargon, if they can't see the color, then all of the information you are attempting to share is lost on them.

Use pictures...if they're relevant

A picture is worth a thousand words. In proposals, especially, the right picture in the right spot can clarify things quickly that it might otherwise take a thousand words to say. Despite this, I offer this admonition: *make your pictures relevant to the topic*!

Once upon a time, I was working with a client that had some ideas about including more pictures in their proposals, and so I asked them to send me the pictures they wanted and where they should be located. The pictures they sent had nothing to do with what we were selling. Their pics of pretty people having a good time would have been great for a beer commercial, but for the business service we were selling, they were completely off topic. They added no value. It was especially problematic because, with the limited page count we had, lots of space was being used up by photos that contributed nothing. Was it more visual? Absolutely. Was it effective? Not even a little bit.

Around the same time, I was working with a client whose business involved spraying chemicals outdoors. They used a special sprayer attachment that prevented overspray, even in windy conditions. This capability is especially important to buyers where water features are involved. We used a picture of the attachment, and included a caption below the picture that explained how its design would minimize or eliminate overspray. This is how pictures should be used. In little more than a glance, the buyer immediately sees that the seller has not only taken steps to minimize overspray, they present an actual device they use to prevent overspray—proof, visual evidence, to support the point.

In proposals, pictures are only effective if they're relevant to the topic.

Infographics

Infographics can be powerful. One of the reasons I like them is because they dramatically improve skimmability. They make it incredibly easy for a proposal reviewer to skim your proposal quickly and understand your message with little additional mental effort.

Most organizations employ at least one person who can create relatively simple infographics on their own. If this is you, I recommend you get these staff members a copy of Mike Parkinson's book, *Do-It-Yourself Billion Dollar Graphics*: *3 Fast and Easy Steps to Turn Your Text and Ideas Into Persuasive Graphics.* For your staff who have artistic abilities, this book will give them the tips and insights to create quality infographics.

Personally, I lack this talent. I'm not only colorblind, I'm spatially inept. Really, seriously, inept. A kindergartner with a box of Crayola® crayons would show me up. If you're like me, if you lack the talent or resources to create these graphics in house, consider hiring a professional. I've found skilled professionals who create infographics for a living create the best infographics. Insightful, eh? But it's true. One experienced infographics professional can consistently outshine a bunch of otherwise talented amateurs with the first brushstroke. These skilled professionals aren't usually inexpensive, but especially if it's an important project, they may well be worth the investment.

CHAPTER RECAP

Businesspeople do not have time to read your proposal, they only have time to skim it. Accepting and embracing this fact, our job as proposal writers is to do everything we can to make our proposals easy for them to skim. Start with these six things:
1. Use lots of headings and subheadings
2. Write concise summaries prior to each answer
3. Introduce each new section with a mini executive introduction
4. Use callout boxes for mini case studies
5. Use callout boxes for quotes
6. Use charts, graphs, and pictures

If a reader can skim your proposal, and still understand your message, you just leapfrogged past the competition.

8. Make Your Proposals Easy to Read

I understand if you're confused. You just finished reading a chapter advocating you make your proposals easy to skim because most people don't read them. Now I'm telling you to make your proposals easy to read, too. So, which is it?

The bottom line is if you want your proposals to be effective, you have to do both. You have to make them easy for people to skim because that's what most people do most of the time. But when a reader finds something she's interested in learning more about, she's going to read your content. When she does, it must be easy for her to read and understand.

> Yes, your proposals must be easy to skim and, yes, they must be easy to read, too.

BE CONCISE—LONG PROPOSALS DO NOT GET READ

"Be concise." This is advice we have all heard from our high school and college instructors when we were learning to write. Today, we may hear the same counsel when tasked with writing a report, presentation, or even an email: *"Please, just keep it short."* In truth, pleas for conciseness are nothing new.

- Voltaire: *The surest way to be boring is to say everything.*
- Antoine de Saint-Exupery: *Perfection is achieved, not when there is nothing more to add, but when there is nothing left to take away.*

Great minds think alike, I suppose, and the common lesson these great minds are both conspiring to teach us is to not say everything, just say the important things. Sometimes detail is important and necessary, and that's OK. Other times, though, it's just too much, or it's irrelevant, or it's redundant–*and it needs to go.*

Most highly-accomplished salespeople understand brevity and relevance—we say what needs to be said and nothing more. When it comes time to write proposals in response to RFPs, however, many of us devolve into a legion of feature preachers. We give into the little voice in the back of our heads that keeps repeating: "More is better, leave nothing out!" We embrace the antithetical philosophy embodied in Tom Sant's infamous "thud factor"—*after dropping all the proposals on a table, the one that makes the biggest thud wins.* In an era where paper is cheap and electrons are cheaper, we respond defiantly to pleas for conciseness by asking a simple question: why say something in one page when we can say the same thing in eighteen?

Why proposal writers are not concise

One of the biggest reasons our answers are so long is because, often, they're Frankenstein answers. Just like Frankenstein was a monster made up of parts from many different souls, our answers are often monsters made up of bits and pieces from previous answers we've written. If you write an answer to a similar question, and then later reuse it in a new proposal, many writers won't take the time to edit out the parts that are not relevant, they just add in some new content that is required. When this happens, the stock answer grows into a monster that's often far longer and uglier than it needs to be. It's a Frankenstein answer.

As we struggle to make our proposals concise, or at least more concise than they are now, precisely how do we do that? What's the secret?

The answer is in two parts. First, making your proposals concise requires planning before you start writing. You have to figure out what you want to say before you sit down to say it. Second, making your proposals concise requires editing what you wrote because chances are good your content doesn't say what you intended to say.

Make a plan before you start writing

When responding to RFPs, one of the things we've all heard numerous times is a salesperson or staff writer say, "We answered a question just like this in the (fill in the name) proposal. Let's plugin that answer here and we're good to go." Grimace.

To be clear, it's OK to start with stock content. If someone asks about your disaster recovery and business resumption strategy, it would be wasteful to write it from scratch every time. What's not OK is using that stock content without customizing it to this buyer and what they care about.

When you are writing an answer to an RFP question, it's important to take time to plan your response, to figure out what you want to say...all *before* putting pen to paper. Over years of doing this, I've discovered that one of the best ways to plan what you want to say is to ask yourself these five questions.

1. Why are they asking this question?

You can't write a good answer if you don't know why they're asking it, or especially if you don't understand the motivation behind it. If you don't know, ask an SME or salesperson in your company to explain it to you—*from the buyer's perspective*. Once you understand, you'll be able to draft a better and more concise answer, and a more targeted benefit statement at the end.

2. How important is this question to their purchase decision?

Sometimes, buyers ask questions because they think they're supposed to, or because they copied it from a previous proposal. In reality, though, their question and your answer are not really that important in their decision process. Other times, how you answer a single question may determine whether you win or lose. Which is it? If you don't know this, you cannot possibly write a compelling proposal.

3. What information do you have to include?

This is key for being concise.

When you review their question, and maybe do a quick outline describing how you want to answer it, be sure to list what information should be included...*and then ignore what shouldn't.* If all they ask for is your disaster recovery plan, don't give them your data backup and business resumption strategy, too. Give them what they ask for and nothing more.

4. Is there a way to structure your response so it reinforces how well you comply with a major requirement or business objective?

The focus of this section is being concise, and that's important. But don't be so focused on being concise that you neglect the things you need to do to make a sale. If they want fantastic customer service, for example, don't just discuss it in response to the question on customer service. It should be a theme that weaves its way throughout your entire proposal.

5. Can you answer this question so it emphasizes one of your strengths? Or ghosts the competition?

Again, the focus of this section is being concise, but don't neglect the opportunity to add some verbiage that differentiates your solution from competing solutions or highlights a competitor's weakness. You never mention a competitor by name, of course, but you can mention the weakness they suffer. See the chapter on differentiators for more explanation on this important topic.

By spending a little bit of time up front to plan your response, you will not only have a better answer, it will also be more concise.

Embrace the editing part of the writing process

The secret to good writing is good editing. I understand most people don't want to hear that. After all, who likes to edit? But the truth is inescapable; if you want clear, concise proposals, you must take the time to make the effort to properly edit your content.

We talk at length about the writing/editing process in a later chapter, and I don't want to duplicate that, here. Still, I want to make the point that the first draft should never, ever be the last draft.

No matter how good a writer you are, what you mean to say in your head isn't always what appears on paper. I've written many things I thought were well written only to discover, on review, my writing was not nearly the award-winning prose I imagined it to be. Some passages might be awkwardly written, too long, too short, or contain numerous misspellings. Other sections might be well written but include contextual errors or even outright falsehoods; unintentional, to be sure, but untrue nevertheless.

Recognizing these realities, it is critical that every proposal be reviewed twice; the first time to make certain the content is accurate, and the second time to make certain your writing is clear, compelling, and consistent with all applicable spelling, grammar, and style rules.

At the end of the day, when all is said and done, we're left with one simple idea: *good writing takes time and effort.* If you invest the time and the effort, your writing will become clearer, more compelling, and more concise.

Living with page limits

Writing concisely is always important, but it's especially important in proposals where we are restricted by page limits. I wish I could offer better advice, a magic wand that would make it easier, but dealing with page limits is difficult. All I can offer are these few tips.

1. Comply with page limits

If the RFP says you have two pages, you have two pages. Don't think it's OK to stretch it to three, and don't try to get sneaky, either. If you choose Arial Narrow font at 10 point font size with narrow margins, you can probably write a novella in two pages, but no one is going to read it (without a magnifying glass). Not only that, your customer will likely become agitated with your attempt to flout their rules.

If you go beyond the RFP's published page limits, if you try to get sneaky, you will be penalized points, create a negative impression of your company, or you may even be disqualified. Don't do it.

2. Plan your response before you write

A couple pages back, there's a section titled, *"Make a plan before you start writing."* The section lists five questions you should ask yourself before you put pen to paper. When you are restricted by page limits, pay special attention to question number three, *"What information do you have to include?"* Specifically, what information is essential and necessary, that you absolutely must include, before the buyer has what he or she needs to be able to say, "OK, they comply."

Though it might be easier to copy and paste an existing answer and then edit it, you'll probably be better served if you write from scratch incorporating only the important things you must include. Write down, in outline form, the main ideas you have to include, and then build your answer around this outline.

3. Visualize how much room you have

When completing a proposal response in a spreadsheet or online submission form where each cell has a specified character limit, try this technique I learned from one of my customers.

This answer is 500 characters. This answer is 500 characters. This answer is 500 characters. This answer is 500 characters. This answer is 500 characters. This answer is 500 characters. This answer is 500 characters. This answer is 500 characters. This answer is 500 characters. This answer is 500 characters. This answer is 500 characters. This answer is 500 characters. This answer is 500 characters. This answer is 500 characters. This answer is 500 characters.

It's a relatively simple technique, but it makes it super easy to visualize how much room you have to work with before you start putting words on paper.

If a section has a page limit, which is what you'll see more often, consider creating a unique document outside of the proposal document, and then mockup the "shell" in that section. The "shell" includes their question and an outline of your answer, complete with answer headings and subheadings.

Again, it's a relatively simple technique, but it aids visualizing how much space you have before you put pen to paper. If you have a five page limit, and your document shell with their question and your outlined response is already one and a half pages, then you have three and a half pages to provide all of your content. It's a way to make you, as one of my clients said, "get real" about how concise you have to get.

4. Offer proof from a credible source

I hate it when a buyer asks a question that legitimately requires lots of detail to answer, but then arbitrarily mandates a page limit that is far too restrictive to provide the information they say they want. In these circumstances, it's almost impossible to fulfill their information request *and* comply with their page limit requirements.

When I find myself in this situation, I do two things. First, I find a way to summarize the information they want as succinctly as possible, and then I evaluate how much space I've used and how much I have available. Depending on how much space is available, I add detail for the topics that I think are most important.

Second, I fortify the summary with some kind of proof or testament from a credible source. I do this because, in my experience, an objective reference or piece of evidence can often replace pages of text trying to explain the same thing. Here are four examples.

We wanted a business jet that was comfortable for long flights. Everyone says their jet delivers this, but most don't. The Business Jet Comfort Association said the ACME Fictional Jet was the best, and our experience supports that statement. Their jets are roomier, quieter, and in general more comfortable than any other jet we've owned or tried.

We worked with many businesses before we started working with Dave's Fictional Company. They have the best customer service we've ever encountered. When they promise, they actually deliver.

We were initially concerned about the reverse phase plutomatic core (RPPC)...is it a real innovation or just a marketing ploy? After using one of their RPPC machines for the last year, we're sold. It's a dependable, reliable machine that has reduced our maintenance costs.

According to the Fictional Insurance Foundation, Dave's Fictional Insurance Company has maintained the highest responsiveness rating of all insurance providers in the Tri-State area. That's an impressive accomplishment.

Page limits are not fun, but they are a fact of life. Figuring out how to sell well despite their sometimes suffocating restrictions will give you an edge over the competition trying to do the same thing.

SHORTER SENTENCES ARE BETTER SENTENCES

I once read a single sentence that was a page and a half long. I was still trying to catch my breath the next morning. It's hard enough getting someone to read our proposals, so where's the sense in scaring them away with a sentence so long that, if read aloud, it would result in certain hypoxia and maybe even temporary unconsciousness?

In the business world, and especially in the proposal world, shorter sentences are better than longer sentences. Ironically, shorter sentences are more difficult and time consuming to write, but they're much easier to read and understand.

Using Flesch-Kincaid to improve readability

There is an ongoing discussion among proposal writers about readability, and specifically, what grade level to write for. They use systems such as the Flesch-Kincaid Grade Level system to assign a readability score to a particular passage or document. The Flesch-Kincaid method starts with sentence length and the average number of syllables per word, and then plugs those into a formula to determine a grade level for a particular document. A passage that receives a grade of 10, for example, is ideal for someone who reads at a 10th grade reading level.

So what grade level should you write for? Many states mandate that insurance policies be written at a 9th grade level. I've heard this level articulated by other business communicators, including some proposal writers. I personally aim to keep my writing in the 10 to 12 range. It's not too basic, but it's not too advanced, either. Moreover, it accounts for some of the technical, multisyllabic words that you can't avoid but that artificially inflate the grade level score of your writing.

Microsoft Word makes it easy to score your writing according to the Flesch-Kincaid method. All you have to do is perform a "Spelling & Grammar" check. If you clicked the option to also check reading level, the check will conclude with a line item that grades the reading level for the document.

Despite this explanation, I advise against getting too caught up in grade-level scoring. It can be educational and enlightening, but it can also become an obstacle if you spend too much time stressing about it. Your primary focus should be writing clearly and concisely, using shorter sentences instead of longer, and using common words instead of their more complex cousins. Do that and everything else will work out.

By the way, the Flesch-Kincaid Grade Level for this section is 9.5. Not bad.

USE JARGON, BUT USE IT *CAREFULLY*

One of the biggest challenges facing most proposal writers is knowing when, where, and how to use jargon.

Contrary to popular opinion, jargon is not bad. In fact, jargon can be a very effective way to communicate complex ideas very efficiently, but it's only effective if the people reading your proposal understand the jargon you're using. This isn't always the case.

In a previous chapter, we discussed how many organizations—state and local government agencies, in particular—will often conscript proposal reviewers from multiple departments. If a city is selecting an employee benefits provider, for example, they may include reviewers from the HR department, finance department, various employee unions, etc. The problem is many of these stakeholders, while generally interested in the benefits program, don't necessarily understand all of the jargon commonly used in the benefits industry. If you use jargon without defining what it means, many of these people will not understand the message you're trying to communicate.

Define jargon in each section

If you're writing a book or magazine article, the generally accepted approach is to define a word or a term one time, and then you're free to use it throughout the rest of the document. It's a good approach because people typically read books and magazine articles sequentially, from beginning to end.

Proposals are different.

People don't usually read proposals sequentially. Many or even most read a proposal like they do a Web page; they bounce from here to there, back to here, and then off again to something else. If you define a term in the first section of your proposal, and then use the same term throughout your proposal, all those people who do not read your proposal sequentially will not understand the meaning of the term.

Therefore, while it is OK to use jargon, it is necessary to define each term and word at the beginning of each section where it's used—or more often if it makes sense. I'd rather risk repeating myself than making a really good argument that influences no one because I'm using words and terms they don't understand.

EXPLAIN EVERY IDEA YOU INTRODUCE

As a professional proposal writer, one of my biggest frustrations is reading proposals in which a writer introduces an idea but doesn't explain it. It's almost as if they expect me to read their minds instead of their words. For example, consider this question and its response:

Q. *Does your office copier have the functionality to collate copies?*

A. *Yes, our copier can collate copies. And unlike most other models, it also includes a reverse phase modulator.*

I can almost hear a fictional reader now. "A what? A reverse phase modulator? What is that? What does that mean? Is that a good thing? How does that impact collating copies?"

The above example is entirely fictional, but I encounter this kind of example all the time. The writer includes an idea that seems important, but doesn't explain *why* it's important. It's the proposal equivalent to an 'end of season' cliffhanger: "Will Batman survive the crushing jaws of the hungry giant eel? Will Robin remember he's a force for good instead of evil? Tune in next week when..."

This approach may work great for nostalgic TV dramas from the 1960s, but it's a horrible way to write a proposal. Seriously. It's hard enough to convince someone to buy what we're selling, we only make it worse when we tempt them with something that seems promising but doesn't explain why it is. It's almost like saying: "I can solve your problem really well, but I'm not going to tell you exactly how. Tune in next week when..." Frustrating!

If you introduce an idea, you must explain it, you must say why it's important, and most of all, you must say why they should care.

CHAPTER RECAP

Though most people skim your proposals quickly, they slow down and read when they find sections they care about. For this reason, you have to make your content easy to read and understand.

1. Be concise—long proposals do not get read
2. Shorter sentences are better sentences
3. Use jargon, but use it carefully
4. Explain every idea you introduce

Part 2: Proposal Process Best Practices

9. Build an Effective Editing and Review Process

In the business world, proofreading and editing are often neglected because busy businesspeople are…*too busy.*

- *We don't have enough people.*
- *We don't have enough time.*
- *We're working on five projects and we only have resources for four.*
- *We're working on six projects and we only have resources for three.*

You get the point.

Against these time and resource pressures, I understand how the proofing and editing functions get neglected. Something has to give, and proofing and editing are usually the easiest tasks to do away with. I don't like it, I don't approve of it, but I understand it.

I've also encountered companies with the exact opposite problem. These companies have too many reviews and reviewers, and the reviewers make so many changes the process devolves into a perpetual editing fiasco. For the poor proposal writer, it's like being accountable to a committee of arguing siblings; Bob wants this but Sally wants that, Sam wants more explanation but Tom wants more pictures. And then there's Albert, the dreaded 11th hour decision maker. Albert will surely have comments and changes, but he won't share these with us until the day before the proposal is due. And Mary? She will say something along the lines of, "This section is weak," but she won't say why it's weak or what, specifically, would make it stronger. Arghhh.

Neither approach works well. In fact, both approaches undermine your efforts to develop a responsive and compliant proposal.

BEST PRACTICE: DEVELOP YOUR OWN EDITING AND REVIEW PROCESS

When you're working on a document as complex and important as a sales proposal—replete with multiple writers, subject matter experts (SMEs), and stakeholders—it's necessary to formalize an effective and efficient process to coordinate everyone's efforts. It has to be your process, and it has to be workable and repeatable. It has to be a normal and routine part of your proposal development effort, not an afterthought that gets addressed 'if you have time.'

That is precisely what this chapter is about.

DON'T WAIT UNTIL THE END TO REVIEW AND EDIT

In many businesses, reviews and proofreading are often performed toward the end. It's almost an afterthought. The problem, of course, is that as you get closer to the deadline, and the pressure is on to get the proposal done and out the door, the necessary reviews and proofing are often minimized or neglected entirely.

This is precisely why I advocate incorporating the editing and review function as an integral part of the proposal development process. So instead of having a proposal writing process over here, and a proposal review and editing process over there, writing and editing/review is integrated into a single process. The biggest advantage of this approach is the heavy editing happens earlier in the process, so the final reviews and edits are more about tweaking and polishing the final product rather than rewriting entire sections.

The proposal development process you develop internally should incorporate at least these four steps.

- Step 1: Create a proposal shell
- Step 2: Source and edit content *before* it gets put into the shell
- Step 3: Review the content
- Step 4: Proof the document

This streamlined, repeatable process will produce better results, more efficiently, in less time.

A word about proposal automation software

Proposal automation software can simplify much of this process; most create the proposal shell automatically, most let you review and approve content before it goes into the working document, etc. In my experience, proposal automation software is a marvelous resource for any business that responds to even a couple RFPs a month.

Just know that the software, to be effective, requires someone to be dedicated to maintaining the system. This person has to ensure that content is continually updated and current, that old content is removed, that new content is reviewed and approved before it goes into the system, etc.

Depending on your proposal volume, a proposal automation system may be an ideal tool for your proposal team. Just be sure you commit sufficient resources to maintaining it or it will become nothing more than "shelfware," software that sits on a shelf that nobody uses.

STEP 1: CREATE A PROPOSAL SHELL

Creating a proposal shell involves taking the sections and questions in the buyer's RFP and then recreating them in your proposal document with your own formatting. This is fairly straightforward but there are a few things to keep in mind.

Copy and paste the customer's questions and numbering scheme verbatim

Buyers almost always group questions into like categories, then they assign a unique numbering scheme to each category and question. For example, a buyer may organize an RFP so all general background questions are in section 1, all technology questions are in section 2, and all quality and customer service-related questions are in section 3. Further, the buyer may number the first question in section 1 as question 1.1, the second question as 1.2, etc.

Buyers organize RFPs this way for a variety of reasons, but top among them is it makes it easier for them to review the responses they receive when all similar questions are grouped together.

When responding to an RFP, it's important to structure your proposal in the same order they are presented in the RFP. For example, if your customer has seven response sections in their RFP, you should have the same seven sections—labeled identically in identical order—in your proposal. If they divide each main section into multiple subsections, you should structure your proposal to reflect this organization.

After the structure is in place, the next step is to copy and paste each of their questions into your shell. This is important. There are few things as difficult as trying to understand an answer without also seeing the question that prompted it. Further—and this is important for proposal writers to understand—the person reviewing your response is not always the same person who wrote the questions. For these people, they need to see your answer within the context of their question.

> Always restate their question prior to your answer, because the people who are reviewing your proposal and reading your answers are not always the same people who wrote the questions.

Now that we're including a question prior to each answer, we need to find a way to clearly differentiate that question from the answer we write.

Questions and answers should have unique formatting

Differentiating their question from your answer makes it easier for them to review your proposal response. There are many ways you can do this.

A different color, like blue, makes it easy for proposal reviewers to easily and quickly differentiate between their question and your answer. It's a common technique, too. But what of those buyers who print your response at their offices? If you submit your proposal electronically, and they print your proposal on a black and white printer, all the text would look alike unless you also use some other distinctive formatting besides color.

In addition to color, therefore, I almost always like to use other formatting that distinguishes the question text. In the following example, the question text is italicized, bold, and the color is adjusted to a lighter gray than the text around it. Compared to the text before and after, it's very easy to distinguish their question from your answer.

1.1 This is an example of one way to format their questions in your proposal. In addition to changing the color of their question, I also recommend changing some other aspect or aspects of the question text. For example, you could format the question in a unique font, a smaller font size, include a light shading behind it, or have it extend a half inch to the left of your answer text. Italic and bold formatting can also be effective.

Here's another consideration. If you are dealing with tight page limits, you might decide to make their question text a smaller font, like 9 or 10 point (depending on the font). You're still restating their question, but you aren't allowing their question to take up your allotted pages.

Dealing with long questions

I love it when a buyer mandates a concise response, but then includes questions that are longer than the entire first chapter of Tolstoy's *War and Peace*! There's nothing wrong with *War and Peace*, by the way, it's just really, really long.

If a question is exceptionally long, you should still restate it prior to writing an answer, but you may choose to summarize it instead of listing it in its entirety. For example, if it takes them half a page to ask for references, then you might summarize their question like this:

3.2.4 Include references who currently use services similar to the ones being sought in this RFP.

Unless they specifically say you have to restate the question in its entirety, this is a perfectly legitimate way to save space and reduce the overall length of your proposal.

Handling multiple part questions

Buyers frequently include questions that have multiple parts in their RFPs. The way you handle these multi-part questions depends on a variety of things, including how many parts there are, how long each answer is, etc.

If there are only two or three parts to the question, I may list the entire question together, then separate each part of my answer with bold headings. If there are more than two or three parts, if each part is unique, or especially if each is part of a bulleted list, I will generally break these questions into multiple sub-questions. For example, I might list the main question in the same way I list all other questions, then I list each sub-question individually followed by its answer. By listing each sub-question with its own answer, it can make it easier for the reviewer to follow and, just as important, to see you've answered each part of each question.

Ultimately, there is no single correct way to answer multipart questions. Just remember our primary goal is to ensure clarity — to make it as easy as possible for the reader to review and understand our response. If you use this goal as your guide, and you invest a bit of time thinking about what format works best, I'm confident you will figure out the best way to organize your response to get the greatest impact.

Write question numbers manually

In the beginning of this section, I described how many RFPs organize questions into sections and subsections. I also explained that many RFPs use numbering schemes such as the one illustrated in the simple example below:

1. Company information
    1.1 How long have you been in business?
    1.2 Where is your headquarters?
2. Customer Service
    2.1 How many customer service staff do you employ?
    2.2 What is your escalation procedure?
    2.3 What is your industry customer service ranking?

In the same way it's important to restate the RFP question before appending your answer, it's also important to include their numbering scheme. This makes it easy for reviewers to quickly locate and review particular answers. For example, if I'm a reviewer, I can send an email to the other reviewers on the team referencing a specific response, *"Hey team, I want to point out ABC's answer to question 2.2 about escalation procedures. I really like their approach, and it's exactly what we're not currently getting from XYZ."*

Here comes the tricky part.

Microsoft Word is today the most commonly used word processing tool in business, and it has a variety of features designed to make life easier for its users. One of these features is automatic numbering. This feature automatically formats a section of text into an outline or multi-level numbering scheme like in the previous example.

Take special note of that word, *automatic*. As I begin each new line of my outline, Word automatically assigns a number in front of it. For example, if I type "1. Introduction, and then hit the Enter key, Word automatically turns this into a numbered list and puts a "2" in front of the next line. If I add questions under section 2, Word automatically labels those as questions 2.1, 2.2, 2.3, etc. It works the other way, too. If I delete question 2.1, Word automatically renumbers everything that follows; question 2.2 would become 2.1, and question 2.3 would become 2.2.

In most circumstances, this is a wonderful feature. If you've got a long, multi-level list and you decide to change the first item in the list, you don't have to worry about changing every number that follows; Word does it for you. In fact, the only time this feature is not great is when you want to maintain a pre-defined numbering scheme—*like when you are building a proposal in response to an RFP!*

It's a problem because any changes you make as you are writing your response might alter the numbering scheme for the entire document. For example, suppose you accidentally deleted "1. Company Information." All of the sections, subsections, and questions would now be numbered differently than the numbering scheme as it appears in their RFP. ***Do you*** *have any idea how much fun it is to discover your entire numbering scheme is incorrect when you only have a few hours left to fix it, print it, and deliver it?* Trust me on this one, it's no fun. In fact, I'm fairly certain all my gray hair—and it is significant—can be traced back to this single feature.

With all this as a background, here is a tip that will simplify your life: *Turn off the automatic numbering feature.*

In the 2010 version of Word, you can do this by clicking on File: Options: Proofing: Autocorrect options, and then make certain the Auto Numbered List checkbox is unchecked. Now you can type "1. Company information," but when you hit enter, it won't automatically turn your text into a numbered list. That's a good thing.

Now that this is done, be sure to manually recreate their numbering scheme in your proposal response.

At this point in the process, you now have a shell of a proposal document. It's time to begin "loading" the document with your content.

STEP 2: WRITE AND EDIT CONTENT **_BEFORE_** IT GETS PUT INTO THE SHELL

Most organizations already create a proposal shell like I described in the previous step. The problem, though, is these same organizations immediately begin "populating" the proposal shell with stock content or content taken from another proposal.

This approach is fundamentally flawed.

It's flawed because you're filling your proposal with answers not written for this opportunity. It's as if you're building a sports car in your garage, but instead of using sports car parts, you're building it with whatever parts you find laying around and then proclaim, "We'll fix it later." You end up with a Frankenstein monster car that may or may not run. It probably looks funny, too.

There's nothing wrong starting with stock content. I do it all the time. But you shouldn't be putting that stock content into your proposal shell until you first edit the content into an answer specific to the opportunity and responsive to the particular question.

> Instead of "populating" the proposal shell with generic content in the very beginning, and then having to edit the entire document later, we should be doing the writing and editing *BEFORE* we put the content into the shell.

This ensures whatever is in the proposal has already been seen, edited, and reviewed at least once.

The importance of having a good writing and editing process

Earnest Hemingway said, "The first draft of anything is shit." Let's begin our discussion by agreeing that Hemingway's assessment, though off color, is essentially correct. Most experienced writers will affirm that the initial draft of anything they write is probably not great. In fact, it often stinks. But that's OK. Stinky is perfectly acceptable for a first draft.

I always find it amazing when I write something and then walk away confident I expressed the message clearly, concisely, and thoroughly. I find it amazing because when I read the passage the next morning, I quickly realize I didn't do nearly as well as I thought. Sometimes, I don't fully explain the ideas I introduce. Other times, I make assumptions about what the reader knows. Frequently, I find grammar and usage errors such as "its" when I meant to say "it's," or "your" when I meant to say "you're." Periodically, I realize there is a much better way to organize the information than how I did it. Ultimately, I don't feel too bad because even professional, world-renowned writers as skilled and talented as Hemingway admit they cannot write well without editing, but it's still humbling.

The good news is, as we implement our new editing process, we can fix these kinds of process-related mistakes and shortcomings, and in their place, implement some writing and editing best practices.

Defining a process for writing and editing content

You get to define your process however you want, but it should at least include these five components:

1. **First author's draft.** The proposal writer works with the SME or salesperson to understand each question and how he should

answer it. The proposal writer then drafts the content and, when done, saves his work and walks away. The proposal writer should not look at what he wrote for at least an overnight.

2. **Second author's draft.** The proposal writer reads the entire draft answer through before making any changes. He then edits the content to address all of the things that make it less than perfect. This is where the heavy editing should occur. He should save his work, walk away, and not look at his document for at least an overnight.

3. **Final author's review.** The proposal writer reads the entire draft through before making any changes. He then makes any minor tweaks or changes, and forwards it to the next step in the process, the SME.

4. **SME review.** The proposal writer gives the draft to the SME (or salesperson or senior manager) for review. Working together, the proposal writer works with the reviewer to make any necessary changes until both are satisfied.

5. **Add the content to the shell.** Only now does the proposal writer add the content to the proposal shell she created in the first step.

Throughout this process, the proposal shell may be incomplete because there are many questions that do not have answers. The good news, though, is what's in there is fairly close to being final; it's already been written, edited, reviewed, and polished by at least two people—one of whom is an SME, salesperson, or senior manager.

Choosing who should write your content

There are few things in the world as difficult and challenging as asking people who are not writers to write something. In fact, I routinely ask students in my proposal classes, "How many of you like to write?" Not many hands come up. Most just chuckle as if I'm asking, "How many of you like getting a root canal?"

I've not done a structured or scientific study on this, but based on the conversations I've had with countless business people, it's clear most don't like writing. They don't like it because it's difficult and time consuming. They say things like, "I don't like writing because it takes too long and I could tell you the same thing—verbally—in a fraction of the time."

Ironically, the thing most non-writers don't know is many professional writers don't like it either. Writing is hard. It's inefficient, too. It can take a long time to take a relatively simple idea and craft it and tweak it and refine it until it's ready for someone else to read.

So how do you teach your SMEs and other staff how to write if they really don't want to? How do you teach them to write well—to be compelling, persuasive, and customer-focused—if they disdain the act of writing so much they push it off until the very last minute?

The answer: *you don't*. You don't ask them to write anything.

Writers write, everybody else supports the writing effort

What role do SMEs and salespeople have in drafting content? This has long been a contentious issue between the sales group, the proposal group, and SMEs. Some argue each of these groups should be intrinsically involved in drafting content, that it's part of their job responsibilities. Others argue they shouldn't be involved at all; after all, they are salespeople and SMEs, not proposal writers.

I've struggled with this question. I've even argued both sides of the issue. After long and careful deliberation, though, I've concluded SMEs and salespeople should not be writing proposal content. There are exceptions, of course—there are always exceptions. If yours is a small company without the significant resources of a huge company like a GE or Boeing, you may not be able to afford a dedicated proposal writer. Indeed, I've been involved in projects where everyone from the president of the company to the receptionist was involved in preparing, writing, editing, reviewing, and assembling a proposal because the company wasn't large enough to have any one person dedicated to the function.

This exception aside, we shouldn't generally be asking our SMEs and salespeople to be writers. Salespeople and SMEs still must be involved in the process—providing guidance, insight, backstories, etc.—but these people are not hired to be writers so let's stop asking them to be something they aren't.

How SMEs, salespeople, and writers can work together

The way content development should work is to make your proposal writers responsible for drafting content, but make certain they have access to the SMEs and salespeople who can help them write the content.

When I'm working on a project, I ask for material I can read to help me understand the subject being discussed. I ask for things like brochures, website content, previous proposal content, and other background stuff.

After reviewing that information, I then meet with the SME or the salesperson to interview him or her about the project. But I don't just say, "What's the answer to this question?" Instead, I typically begin with my own question that helps me to understand better: "In the RFP, this is what they say they want. Why are they asking for this?" Then I utter a phrase that I've become famous for among many of my clients, "Teach me!" This basic question is usually followed by many others:

- Why did they ask it *this* way?
- Why do they care?
- What do they want to accomplish?
- Why does this matter?"
- What's the significance?
- Is this unique from what our competitors are doing?

The "teach me" approach is not just about answering this one question, it's about understanding the bigger picture. It's about understanding what the customer needs, what they want, and how we can help them get it. Once I have this understanding, I have what I need to write an answer that is compelling, persuasive, and specific to this client's needs. This is what proposal writers everywhere should be doing; instead of just trying to answer questions, we should be seeking to understand. Then, over time, we will be able to answer more questions on our own—in a sense become our own SMEs—and ultimately, provide more value to our companies.

STEP 3: THE FINAL CONTENT REVIEW

Fast forward three weeks. What we've accomplished so far is to create a proposal shell filled with content written and edited specifically for this opportunity. It's not a final version, but it's getting close. Everything that's in there has been written specifically for this opportunity and the specific questions posed, it's been edited for clarity and accuracy, and each answer has been individually reviewed and accepted by internal experts or the salespeople involved in the project.

Up until now, we've been slogging around in the muck, focusing on the trees instead of the forest. We've been working to make our answers correct and technically accurate, persuasive, focused on the specific needs of this buyer, and making sure each answer actually answers each question.

Now is the time to take a step back and look at the forest instead of just the trees, to look at the proposal in its entirety. That means performing a content review of the entire proposal.

Who should be involved in the content review?

There should be two roles in the content review phase of the proposal development process; the reviewers and the decision maker.

Content reviewers

Content reviewers could be the team members involved in the project, a subset of this team, and perhaps one or two other people in the organization who have demonstrated a knack for making good content suggestions. Personally, I prefer a smaller group of well-qualified people rather than a larger group. A smaller group of well-qualified people will still find the important things to address, but you're also going to limit the volume of changes to what's most relevant. That's always good.

Whoever you choose to involve in the review, make certain they have the personality and demeanor to offer substantive feedback. Some people offer little more than nitpicky suggestions or comments; they do little more than reword sentences or suggest different words that make no substantive difference to the final product. Ultimately, they consume lots of time without adding much value.

Decision maker

There needs to be one person—a senior manager with the authority to make decisions—who is responsible for considering the reviewers' comments and suggestions and, ultimately, choosing how to handle each one.

Having a single decision maker is important. I've been involved in reviews where there were so many reviewers, often with conflicting views, that building a consensus was difficult. At the very least it was overly time consuming. A single decision maker solves this problem. After everyone has their say, this person has the authority to say, "OK, good feedback. Thanks everyone. Now here's what I've decided."

Putting structure to the review process

I read an article posted by Carl Dickson, founder of CapturePlanning.com, now PropLIBRARY.com. In the article, Carl suggests that instead of asking people for their comments when reviewing a proposal, we should be asking for their instructions. It's a simple idea, but it's brilliant!

Too many times, I get generic or non-specific feedback that does little or nothing to help me make improvements. I remember one comment, in particular, where the reviewer offered, "This section is weak." Arghhh. This does not help me. I don't even know what this means.

- Where is it weak?
- Why is it weak?
- Is the whole thing weak or just some parts?
- What can I do to make it better?

If we take Carl's advice, though, we don't give reviewers the option of making these kinds of useless and non-actionable observations. By asking them for their instructions, we're challenging them to think through the changes they actually want made. This is so much better, and so much more productive, than trying to figure out what is meant by, "this section is weak."

The other major benefit of Carl's approach is it forces a reviewer to think through what he or she wants to say before sharing a comment that might be dispiriting to others on the team. Having spent lots of time in the trenches, I can tell you it's difficult to spend so much brain power stressing about the message, the best way to articulate it, and the specific words to convey it, and then get a punch in the gut when someone who hasn't been through all of that offhandedly states, "this section is weak." Even the best and most righteous among us want to strike back; "Yea, but you're ugly. And so are your kids!" In a high stress environment like proposal development, this kind of off-handed comment is demoralizing.

Now, all that said, I'd still happily speak with someone who plops down on the other side of the desk and says something like, "Look, I've read it. I've considered it. I think it's weak, but I can't tell you specifically what to do to make it better. Can we talk it through?" Yes! I'd love that kind of interaction because it not only achieves the same goal—building a better proposal—it is in many ways more effective because the situation has now evolved into two professionals working together to "build a better mousetrap." Ideally, this dialogue would happen early in the process. Realistically, it happens when it happens. Either way, the product of the dialogue is going to produce lots of good stuff; better proposal content, a better understanding of the issues by the proposal writer, improved camaraderie among team members, etc.

Either way, just don't say, "Give me your comments, please." Structure the kind of information you want back and you're going to have better, more actionable information to work with. Thanks, Carl.

Defining the kind of feedback you want

When you hand off the proposal to your content review team, encourage them to focus their reviews on five questions.

1. Do we clearly articulate that we understand the customer's issues, challenges, or objectives?

In the kickoff meeting we hold prior to the proposal development phase—which we discuss in depth in subsequent chapters—we spend lots of time discussing what the buying organization and the individual decision makers want. It is smart that we do this. After all, it's only by providing them what they want that they'll be interested in what we offer.

- Do we clearly articulate that we understand their issues/challenges/objectives?
- Do we address their interests only in one location or do we reference them throughout the proposal?
- Do we use their own words and phrases to describe what they want?

These are just a few examples, but you get the point. Is the proposal about them, the buyer?

2. Do we articulate our solution effectively?

In addition to acknowledging their issues, challenges, or objectives, do we effectively articulate how our solution is going to help them get what they want? It's not about us and what we want, it's about how we can help them get what they want. Do we make that clear?

3. Do we answer the questions that are asked?

This is an issue I encounter frequently with many proposals I review; you do a really good job structuring a really good answer, but ultimately, it doesn't answer the question being asked. So as you're reviewing your proposal, you need to be asking, are you actually answering the question that was asked?

4. Is there anything that stands out as being technically incorrect?

We've already done some major writing and editing work, and an SME or salesperson has reviewed each answer before we entered it into the proposal. Still, with all that heavy lifting, it's entirely possible even one of your experts can overlook something important.

5. Is the proposal persuasive and compelling?

If you were the reader, would you be swayed by the message we are communicating? Would you find it compelling. Are you thinking to yourself, "I should choose these guys!"

STEP 4: PROOFREADING REVIEW

After the content review is completed, and the decision maker has considered and made a decision about each comment, the content edit window closes. At this point, no more content edits are allowed or permitted. And while this may frustrate those reviewers who wait until the last minute, most notably the dreaded *11th hour decision makers*, it's an essential step for improving the overall effectiveness of the proposal development and review process.

At this stage, the only thing left to do is to assign the proposal to a proofreader.

Find a good proofreader

A good proofreader is amazing. He or she will find things that everyone else on the team overlooks. This includes misspelings, Inconsistencies, extra extra words and missing , grammar error's, punctuation errors; issues with page numbers, font irregularities, etcetera, etc., and more etc. In addition to finding all of these errors, he's worth his weight in gold when he finds the killer errors—like when you spell the customer's name incorrectly.

You can either engage a contract proofreader to perform this function or, if you have the resources, hire a full-time in-house proofreader. If you're a small company, if you don't have the financial resources to contract with or hire someone, look internally for someone who has the proofreading skills you need.

I find accountants often make excellent proofreaders because they're very detail-oriented. But make sure you look around because you may find them in the most unlikely places: a receptionist, someone in the mail room, a person in your call center who has an English degree. If you look, I suspect you'll find talented people who are perfect for the proofreading role who are hiding in plain sight.

Regardless where you find a proofreader, do not, do not, do not skip this step. It's that important.

CHAPTER RECAP

Different companies implement different review processes based on the complexity of their proposal development process and their access to resources. Large corporations have comprehensive review programs.

Small businesses have far more limited programs they build from what resources are available.

You build it in whatever way works best for you. The only two rules are you must build it, and it must be workable so it is used on every proposal development project.

10. Post-Procurement Research and Analysis

In all likelihood, the reason you're reading this book is because you respond to RFPs and you want to win more of them. Or maybe you're tired of losing too many of them. Either way, you want to get better and improve your win rate.

There's all kinds of advice in this book to help you do many things better, but realistically, you can't implement everything at once; there's too much. So how do you prioritize your efforts? How do you know what's most broken, what's in most need of attention? That's what this chapter is about.

If you follow the advice in this chapter, if you regularly perform post-procurement research and analysis, you will learn both what you're doing well and where you're falling short. Then you'll know where to focus your attention.

If you're serious about getting better, if you're serious about winning more opportunities more often, you should understand, embrace, and then implement the best practices articulated in this chapter.

DO AN INTERNAL "LESSONS LEARNED" REVIEW

I recommend beginning each post procurement evaluation by interviewing the people involved in your proposal development effort. This includes everyone: sales, SMEs, proposal writers, and even the person who prints and assembles each proposal. Make certain you create a safe environment where they can speak freely, where they're safe from retribution. Then ask them for their honest opinions.

- What worked and what didn't?

- Which processes could work better? Which could be eliminated?
- Is a process unduly complicated? How can we make it better?
- Did we address the customers problems or did we just talk about ourselves?
- Are SMEs truly available to proposal writers or are they too disconnected from the process?
- Is one person dominating the entire effort or are all encouraged to participate?

These are just a few questions to get you started, but take care not to make your interviews too structured. Let them flow where people want to take them.

Your employees know a lot. Listen to them. Learn from them. All you have to do is ask.

REQUEST COPIES OF COMPETITIVE PROPOSALS

If you are bidding on state and local government projects—*this does not apply to commercial projects*—you should always request copies of your competitors' proposals. It's a simple idea; if you have the opportunity to read their proposals, you gain insight into the message they're sharing with the buyer. You also learn what they think their competitive advantage is and, if you're lucky, how they're positioning themselves against you. Clearly, this is good information to have; it's the kind of intelligence that is actionable in future sales pursuits.

Many organizations don't request competitive proposals because they either don't know they can or they don't know how. In fact, you do have a legal right to request this information from the federal government and in each of the 50 states. Further, most state agencies are so used to processing these requests that they won't think twice about your request. It's normal and routine for them.

Here's a brief background if you aren't already aware.

The federal government passed a law called the Freedom of Information Act, commonly referred to as FOIA. It allows anyone to request information from executive branch agencies. There are some limitations to what you can request. For example, they won't provide information that is confidential (they won't give you battle plans), private information on individuals (you can't request someone's personal tax return), etc. You can, however, request copies of proposals that vendors have submitted in response to RFPs.

The reason I'm introducing FOIA here is because it's a term sellers may hear from time to time, and it's often used colloquially whenever a company is requesting competitive proposals from a state agency: *"When we're done with this procurement, let's FOIA the other proposals to see what our competitors proposed."*

Requesting state records

State and local governments (including publicly-owned schools) are not subject to FOIA. Despite this, each state has its own open records laws that function essentially the same way. You can request all kinds of information—including proposals—just by asking and following their request guidelines.

Each state has its own process for requesting records. The good news is the National Freedom of Information Coalition has done a good job compiling all of this distributed information into a single place. Their website, www.nfoic.org, is a great resource that can help you through the process.

You can limit what buyers share with your competitors

Though it's relatively easy to use open record laws to get copies of your competitors' proposals, some sections of their proposals may be redacted or not included in the package you receive. This is because most state laws allow sellers to protect sensitive or proprietary content by labeling it confidential. This is precisely why most RFPs include verbiage that says something along the lines of, "The responder must indicate any section of this proposal that you consider confidential." If you request copies of all of the proposals submitted for a particular bid, you will typically receive everything except for the sections the other sellers labeled as confidential.

Now turn this around. If you submit a proposal, but you do not label anything as confidential, your competitors will get everything—your pricing, contact information for your most talented and experienced employees, the recipe to your secret sauce, contact information for your best reference customers, etc.

Though you should leverage this privilege to protect the confidential and proprietary components of your bid, be reasonable. You can't get away with labeling your entire proposal as confidential, and most agencies will push back if you try to protect too much. In fact, it can even work to your detriment; if you claim everything is confidential, some courts may invalidate your claim leaving you with no protection. Therefore, make the effort to protect the important stuff that really does qualify as confidential and proprietary, but stop there. Depending on what you're selling, you may want to engage an attorney on this point to make sure you are doing it correctly.

Analyzing other vendors' proposals

In many respects, getting other vendors' proposals sent to you is the easy part. The hard part is figuring out what to do with them once you get them.

I recommend you do two things. First, name them and store them so they're accessible by everyone. Second, assign someone to summarize them.

Name them and store them

When you submit a request to receive copies of all of the proposals submitted in response to an RFP, you will most likely receive them in electronic format. In fact, this is one of the primary reasons, when responding to RFPs, that buyers require you submit your proposal in electronic format; they want your electronic copy so they can more effectively respond to freedom of information requests.

If you are good about requesting competitive proposals following each procurement, recognize you are going to be very shortly inundated with competitive proposals. Therefore, you need to find a way to log and store them on some kind of shared drive so you can review them today and retrieve later.

You get to decide how you want to log them and store them. However you do it, just make certain the proposals you store are available to your business development staff and they're organized in a way that makes them easy to find.

Summarize proposals and then share the summaries

When a company is writing a proposal in response to an RFP, they're typically trying to put their best foot forward, make the best possible impression, advance their most persuasive arguments. As a consequence, proposals typically represent some of the best competitive intelligence you're going to find—*anywhere*. In the sales world, getting access to a competitor's sales proposal is like finding a pot of gold. It only makes sense, then, to squeeze out every bit of knowledge and insight you can.

Here's the problem. If you give everyone in your business development organization—including salespeople, proposal writers, subject matter experts, and other managers—a stack of 100-page proposals, no one is going to read or analyze them. There's just too much work to do and not enough time to do it.

Therefore, I recommend you assign one astute, competitive-minded person to review and analyze the competitive proposals you receive from each procurement. This person's mission is to prepare a summary for each proposal. Each summary should be organized similarly so all reviewers get used to the same format. Organize your summaries in whatever way makes most sense to your business, but consider starting with these sections:

1. General summary of the overall effectiveness of the bid.
   a. Did it win the bid?
   b. Was it compelling?
2. Solution summary
   a. Describe the quality or effectiveness of the solution that was proposed.
   b. Is there anything the bidder proposed that we didn't expect?
   c. Is there anything new they're offering that they haven't in the past?

      d.   What features or capabilities do they write about that are relevant and that our team should know about?

3. Proposal summary
   a. Is their proposal impressive? Weak? Average?
   b. Does their proposal look professional?
   c. Are there any techniques or concepts that we could use in our own proposals?

4. Strengths and weaknesses
   a. What specific strengths do they articulate?
   b. Are there any apparent weaknesses that we can exploit?

5. Competitive assessment
   a. How do they position themselves in the market?
   b. How do they position themselves against us?
   c. Are they launching any new products or initiatives we should be aware of?
   d. Is there any evidence they ghosted our company or solution?

6. Opportunities to exploit
   a. Are there any apparent opportunities we may want to exploit in the future?
   b. Are there any ideas or concepts, or ways of expression, we might want to adopt?
   c. Are there any people on their staff we may want to consider hiring if the need arises in the future?
   d. Is there any new information about the buyer that we didn't know before and that may be useful in the future?
   e. In the references section, or in quotes throughout the body of the proposal, do they reference buyers from other agencies or companies? Do our salespeople know these people?

Again, you can organize your summaries in whatever way makes most sense to you, just make certain you standardize on one structure and stick with it.

Choose which proposals to summarize

Having access to unique summaries for each of your competitors' proposals would be awesome, but let's be realistic, who has the time? Depending on how many procurements you pursue, you'd have to hire an entire staff just to write post-RFP proposal summaries. That would be a waste of resources.

Therefore, spend time beforehand figuring out which procurements and proposals are critical and will generate the most insights. This way, you can learn from the intelligence you collect, but still minimize the investment you make in the effort.

Share your findings

In my experience, some companies that invest in this effort don't always do a great job sharing what they've found or make the best use of the information they uncover. I recommend you make a concerted effort to change that.

First, whenever a staff member completes a post RFP proposal summary, email the link to all of the people who were on the team responding to the proposal, as well as others in your company who may be interested in reading the information the review uncovered. This may include salespeople and sales managers, subject matter experts, proposal writers, program managers, company managers, etc.

Second, encourage the managers of each department—sales managers, proposal mangers, etc.—to raise the summary in their next staff or sales meeting, and discuss what their staff learned from the information. "Bob, what did you think of the summary of the XYZ procurement we got last week?"

The information gained is only valuable if people learn from it and, sometimes, the only way to get people to make the effort to learn from it is to challenge them to do it.

DOING A DEEP DIVE, PERFORMING AN ANSWER-BY-ANSWER COMPARISON AGAINST A COMPETITIVE PROPOSAL

One of my customers was telling me about a competitive challenge his company was struggling with; they were placing second far too often whenever they were bidding against a particular vendor. Most of us have been in this situation at one time or another, but even if you haven't, it's easy to recognize how frustrating it would be.

What they decided to do was to perform an in-depth analysis comparing and contrasting their proposal against the competitor's proposal. They took it seriously, too, as evidenced by the time they invested in the effort.

First, they got a copy of the competitor's proposal. Then they commandeered a board room with two projectors. On one screen was their proposal and on the other screen was their competitor's proposal. He reported it took them a day and a half to complete the effort, but as a team, they reviewed each response to each question. They considered how each proposal was scored, they took notes about ways to improve their response, and they identified areas in their proposal that were deficient.

Obviously, this sort of deep dive is time consuming, and it's probably not a process most small businesses could afford to do more than occasionally. Still, I can't imagine any other effort that would reveal as much understanding about your position relative to a specific competitor.

Management could learn something from this exercise

This exercise should provide excellent insights for anyone in business development, but I can't help thinking how advantageous it would be for senior managers.

Senior managers aren't always involved in day-to-day selling efforts, so imagine if your company's senior managers had the opportunity to spend a couple days in a meeting reviewing exactly what your competitors are saying about themselves and their solution—*and about your company.* They'd see your strengths, to be sure, but they'd also see all of your warts and blemishes and shortcomings.

Depending on your managers, and how willing they are to seriously consider the facts, to learn what's really going on out in the selling trenches, it might be time well spent.

PERFORM POST-DECISION INTERVIEWS WITH BUYERS

Post RFP interviews, sometimes referred to as debriefs, are common in the federal world but they are relatively uncommon in the commercial and non-federal government markets. In fact, I find it striking that, in the many years I've been in the proposal consulting field, I've worked with only a few companies who take the time and make the effort to debrief with the buyer following a procurement.

It is so striking because organizations that respond to RFPs on a regular basis can learn so very much by interviewing buyers after a procurement is concluded. You can learn what you did well, what you did not do well, whether your message was well received, their perception of your competitive position, and much more. For organizations serious about improving their proposal success rate, there are few methods that allow you to collect information as quickly as you can through buyer interviews.

Drafting a post-RFP interview

After an organization makes a commitment to conduct post-RFP customer interviews, the biggest challenge is often knowing what questions to ask. Because we spend so much time working on our proposal, our inclination is to focus our questions around the proposal. The problem is your customer doesn't just evaluate the way you've written your proposal, they evaluate the effectiveness of your solution, the price, the quality and appropriateness of the references you provide, the relevance of your experience to the current project, your credibility, etc. They also compare your overall offering to those being proposed by your competition. Said another way, if we consider the project from the customer's perspective, and we tailor our survey to reflect that, we're going to get a comprehensive and insightful understanding of our competitive position as well as the overall quality of our solution.

Before contacting any customer, therefore, it's important to draft a post-RFP survey that captures the most important and relevant information. I recommend drafting a master survey that includes both standard questions along with sections that are customized to reflect the specifics of each opportunity. Further, I recommend that you organize your questions into five key areas: proposal effectiveness, solution effectiveness, price, your qualifications, and your competitive position.

Here is a list of example questions you may choose to ask.

General questions
1. Please describe your overall impression of the solution we proposed.
2. Please describe your impression of how well our solution addressed your organization's needs.
3. Was there anything about our solution that you particularly liked?
4. Was there anything about our solution that you did not like?
5. Why did you choose <<name of the winning vendor>>?
6. Was there one thing, or multiple things, that counted for us (or against us)?

Price questions
1. In our proposal, we attempted to distinguish between the initial cost of our product and the total cost of ownership. Was this argument clear to you?
2. Did our total cost of ownership discussion have any bearing on your decision?
3. Overall, did you perceive our price to be competitive?
4. Compared to other respondents, was our price among the lowest, among the highest, or somewhere in the middle?
5. Ultimately, how important was price in your decision?

Qualification questions
1. Your RFP listed a variety of qualifications and minimum requirements. In your view, how well did we satisfy these requirements?
2. Were there any specific instances in which we did not meet minimum requirements?

Competitive position questions
1. Did you rank respondent proposals? If so, where did we fall in that list? For example, did we come in #2, #3, or last place?

2. Our program is fully automated. Our competitors programs are either partially automated or completely manual. We worked hard in the proposal to emphasize this difference. Was this distinction clear to you? If so, was this distinction relevant to your decision process?

3. We understand you selected <<name of the winning vendor>>. Was it a difficult decision or were they the clear winner?

4. If a difficult decision, what were the issues you struggled with?

5. If they were the clear winner, what caused them to rise above the others?

6. We understand you selected <<name of the winning vendor>>, who had the contract previously. This is certainly common; most vendors choose the incumbent the majority of the time. My question to you is, under what circumstances would you have selected a new vendor over the incumbent? Was there something specific you were looking for? Was the case from other vendors just not compelling enough?

Proposal effectiveness questions

1. In general, what was your perception of our proposal?

2. Was there anything about our proposal you particularly liked?

3. Was there anything about our proposal you did not like?

4. Is there anything we can do in future proposals to improve them or make them more helpful to you?

5. You read a lot of proposals. We write a lot of proposals, and like everyone, we want to get better. Is there anything about the proposals you read—likes, dislikes, frustrations, aspirations—that you would change if you could?

I am not suggesting you use these questions; they're just examples to start the creative juices flowing. You should come up with your own list of standard questions. You can throw in a few questions that are opportunity specific, but make sure most of them are standardized. This way, you can compare your progress going forward.

Rules about conducting a post-RFP interview

When you ask a buyer to participate in a post-RFP interview, there are a number of rules with which you must comply. Listed here are the most important.

Interviews, not questionnaires

I recommend scheduling interviews with buyers rather than sending them questionnaires to complete. There are three reasons for this. First, you are asking a buyer or client to invest their time in helping you to improve your proposal process. It's unprofessional to ask them to do all the work. Second, your response rate is going to be low if you do a questionnaire because, on their own, most people won't find the time or be willing to work to complete it. Finally, you aren't going to capture the gems of information that you would otherwise get through an interactive interview.

When you are conducting an interview and the buyer says something interesting, interviews give you the freedom to explore those things in more depth...

> *"OK, this is great information, but I want to follow up to something you said. You said your team felt we didn't fully comply with your minimum requirements. Can you talk more about that? I'd like to understand where we fell short."*

The ability to follow up to a comment with another question is often necessary to get a full and comprehensive understanding.

Choose the right people to interview

If at all possible, it is best to interview the person in the buyer's organization who has senior, line management, decision making authority. Sometimes, you don't always have that option; they let you talk with a contracting officer and that's all you get. Ask the question, though, and sometimes you'll get lucky.

Never argue

When the buyer answers a question, it is permissible to ask a clarifying question if you do not fully understand their answer or if you want to dig deeper. However, it is not permissible to argue. The purpose of this interview is to understand their perception of your proposal and your message, not challenge the conclusions they have made. If you argue, you will necessarily put them on the defensive, and they will likely stop cooperating, or at the very least, the feedback they provide will be less than relevant.

Set the tone

When scheduling an interview, it's important to put the buyer at ease. One of the biggest concerns that most procurement people have, especially those associated with state or local governments, is that the seller will file a protest that challenges the fairness of a decision. If the buyer even suspects you might be looking for information to support a protest, the information you collect will be generic, nonspecific, and generally irrelevant. In contrast, if the buyer recognizes your primary goal is to improve the quality of the proposals you produce, to gain insight, then he or she will be more willing to provide meaningful and relevant feedback. There are always a few that will be reluctant, of course, but most of the people you talk with will be accommodating.

When scheduling an interview, therefore, I like to begin by making a clear statement:

> *Our purpose for requesting this interview is to improve the quality of the service we sell and the proposals we produce. We're trying to improve. Therefore, everything we discuss is "off the record."*

Most procurement people will be more willing to share their insights—honestly and openly—if you are open and honest with them about your intentions.

The caveat to this, of course, is you can't file a protest afterward, no matter what you learn. Make sure you're good with that before moving forward.

Choose your interviewers carefully

For larger organizations, I often recommend hiring a management consulting firm, a market research firm, or a proposal consulting firm that has the capability to conduct client interviews on your behalf. Using a third-party firm can often produce better quality results because the buyer is not worried about offending the seller with whom she's been working; she feels free to speak more openly.

While this approach is generally preferable, not every organization can afford to work with a third-party organization to perform post-RFP interviews. Despite this, small and midsize businesses that choose to perform post-RFP interviews themselves can still collect a treasure trove of valuable and important information.

It is important to choose someone within your organization who has the skills and ability to perform a good interview. At a minimum, the person you choose must be personable and easy to talk with, familiar with the product or service you provide, familiar with the market including your competitors, and familiar with the types of problems and issues that your customers typically face.

In general, it is best if your interviewer is not the salesperson who has been working with the buyer, or the person who actually wrote the proposal. These people are generally too close to the opportunity to be objective, and are more likely to take negative feedback personally. An objective, knowledgeable, third party will typically collect better and more meaningful information, and ask better follow up questions, than someone who is too personally connected to the project.

DEVELOP METRICS TO TRACK YOUR PERFORMANCE

Businesspeople are fond of goals. We routinely define sales goals, production goals, customer service goals, market share goals, and more. This is good because goals serve an important purpose; they give us something to aim for. Especially in distributed organizations, goals are an effective way to get everyone working in unison towards a shared vision.

The problem is while we spend a significant amount of time focusing on our goals—where we want to end up—we don't always spend enough time or effort figuring out where we are today. That's a problem, and it's precisely where performance metrics can help us.

Performance metrics are an excellent way to quantitatively measure the effectiveness of an organization's proposal program as it is today.

After calculating this baseline, these metrics are also an excellent tool for measuring progress. After all, making changes to your existing processes are useless unless you can be certain the changes you've made result in better outcomes.

In general, I recommend calculating eight ratios:

- Gross win ratio
- The short list and presentation win ratios
- The incumbent and new business development ratios
- The RFP response ratio
- The shot in the dark proposal response and proposal win ratios.

In addition to calculating these ratios for your business, I also recommend calculating these ratios for each line of business, target market, or whatever other groupings you use. For example, you may calculate the incumbent win ratio for your entire business, but then separately calculate the same ratio for the Western division and the Eastern division. This gives you a more granular view of how well you're doing.

Gross win ratio

The gross win ratio is the most basic and fundamental of all RFP-related win rates. The Gross Win Ratio is calculated by dividing the total number of RFP opportunities that you've won by the total number of RFPs to which you've responded. For example, if you responded to 100 RFPs and you won forty, then you divide 40 by 100 to come up with a win ratio of 40%.

This high-level ratio offers an easy way to measure the overall effectiveness of your proposal efforts. Its shortcoming, though, is it's too general to provide much actionable information. For example, if your Gross Win Ratio is 40% but all you've been doing is pursuing incumbent opportunities, I'd be concerned because 40% is lower than I'd expect. If your gross win rate is 40% but all you've been doing is pursuing new opportunities, then you're probably doing something right because, in this scenario, 40% is a huge number.

The point is the gross win rate may give you a big picture view, but it's too general to offer actionable intelligence.

Short list win ratio & presentation win ratio

In many industries, buyers who issue RFPs don't select vendors based solely on the proposals they submit but instead use a two-step selection process. In the first step, the buyer evaluates the proposals that are submitted by each vendor. From these proposals, the buyer then selects the two or three vendors they most prefer. In the second step, the preferred sellers are invited onsite to deliver a presentation to the people who will be making the ultimate buying decision.

Among people who respond to RFPs, this is often called "making it to the short list."

Understanding this process is important for any organization focused on improving the effectiveness of their proposal efforts. It means your overall success is not based solely on the quality or content of your proposal, it's also based in part on your ability to effectively present your solution in person.

I was contacted one day by a senior sales manager who wanted to arrange proposal training for her staff. Their win ratio, she explained, was far below what they thought it should have been. As we spent more time exploring their proposals and proposal process, however, it became clear that the problem was not their proposals. In the majority of cases, the proposals they wrote were highly effective at advancing them to the short list. The problem we discovered was their presentations; they were not effective at presenting their solution onsite. Said another way, they didn't need proposal training, they needed presentation skills training.

This story illustrates the importance of measuring your performance at a more granular level than what can be done with the gross win ratio, alone. By measuring performance at each stage of the process, you gain a more precise understanding of what you're doing well and what you might need to improve. This is precisely what the short list win ratio and the presentation win ratio are designed to capture.

- The short list ratio is calculated by dividing the number of times you make it to the short list divided by how many proposals you submit in response to RFPs. For example, if you submit 100 proposals and you advance to the short list 75 times, then you divide 75 by 100 to come up with a short list win ratio of 75%.

- The presentation win ratio is calculated by dividing the number of opportunities you win by the number of times you make it to the short list. For example, if you win 25 opportunities, and you made it to the short list 50 times, then you divide 25 by 50 to come up with a presentation win ratio of 50%.

In contrast to the gross win ratio which only gives us a very high-level view of the effectiveness of our business development efforts, calculating the short list win ratio and the presentation win ratio gives us a much more precise understanding of what's working and what isn't.

Incumbent and new opportunity ratios

Your win rate is going to vary dramatically based on whether you are the incumbent or the competition. If you are the incumbent, your win ratio should generally be higher—between 70% and 90%. If you are the competition, your win rate will likely be lower—between 5% and 15%, or between 30% and 40% if you're really good.

Therefore, if you want an accurate assessment of how well you are doing, more accurate than what is reflected in the gross win ratio alone, it is important to delineate between re-bids to existing clients and new bids to new clients.

- The incumbent ratio is calculated by dividing the number of opportunities you win from existing clients by the number of proposals you submit.
- The new client ratio is calculated by dividing the number of opportunities you win from new clients by the number of proposals you submit.

By distinguishing between incumbent opportunities and new business opportunities, you are able to build a much more accurate model of your overall business development performance.

RFP Response Ratio

I often work with managers who believe that every RFP represents an opportunity, and therefore, it's their responsibility to respond to each and every one they receive. I wholeheartedly, passionately, and without reservation, completely disagree with this approach. While it is true every RFP represents an opportunity, it's also true that not every opportunity is a good opportunity. Or a winnable opportunity.

Consider the case of a small, three-person Web development firm. In the twelve months they've been in business, the three founders have racked up a noteworthy collection of clients and an impressive body of work. They've done an excellent job networking in the local business community, and people are starting to take notice of their fledgling firm. Then one day they receive an RFP, out of the blue, from a local but very large multinational corporation. The RFP describes a project that seems to be a great fit for what they do, but it involves developing and supporting a corporate-wide Web application that will be rolled out globally. Should they respond?

I've been in sales my whole life and, as a result, any opportunity I encounter gets my adrenaline pumping and my heart racing. Therefore, I'd probably make an effort to learn more about the opportunity, and specifically, why they chose to send the RFP to us. Barring some unusual findings, though, I would probably advise this client not to respond to this RFP for three reasons. First, all their customers to date have been local businesses under 250 employees. Their lack of experience working with a major multinational corporation is a significant hurdle that would be difficult to overcome. Second, they had no contact with this firm prior to receiving the RFP. The only information they have is what's presented in the RFP, and that generally isn't enough to thoroughly understand and qualify an opportunity. Third, with only three people in the firm, they lack the infrastructure that a major, multinational organization would certainly be looking for in an organization they will rely on to support a global application. Unless the three of them have nothing to do for the next few weeks and they're looking for something to pass the time, they have no business responding to this RFP.

As all of us know, though, business decisions aren't always so well-reasoned and logical. Bolstered by their recent successes, all they see when they look at this particular RFP is a huge opportunity, lots of dollar signs, and a short cut to the big leagues. So they respond. Then they lose.

This story is entirely fictional, but it's not made up.

In a traditional face-to-face sales process, professional salespeople "qualify" an opportunity to determine whether it is a good fit for both the seller and the buyer—before they invest additional resources. The problem that we run into with RFPs—and that we're going to discuss in more detail in a later chapter—is that sellers don't always qualify an RFP opportunity as diligently as they otherwise would if it were not associated with a formal procurement.

As a result, many sellers have a tendency to respond to every RFP they receive, even those they would otherwise disqualify if they were to review the opportunity more thoroughly. The result is the seller invests lots of resources into opportunities they aren't going to win.

The purpose of the RFP response ratio is to measure how discriminating a company is in determining which RFPs to pursue. It's calculated by dividing the total number of RFPs that are pursued by the total number of RFPs that are received.

By itself, the RFP response ratio is not the most insightful piece of information you'll ever collect. If you respond to 100% of the RFPs you receive, for example, it could mean you aren't being very discriminating in how you use your resources. However, it could also mean that of the RFPs you've received, each was a good fit for your company. In other words, an optimal response ratio could be 50% for one business and 100% for another.

The value of the RFP response ratio is not the statistic, itself; it's the awareness it creates among managers about how internal resources are being used. For managers who automatically respond to every RFP they receive, the RFP response ratio encourages them to invest time thinking about whether an individual RFP represents a legitimate opportunity that is winnable, or whether it's a poor fit that will more than likely result in a failed bid and much wasted time.

Shot in the dark ratios

Imagine you are standing in an open field in the middle of the night holding an official Daisy® Red Ryder BB gun (be careful, you'll shoot your eye out). Ten yards away, hidden in the inky darkness of night, there is a soda can resting atop a log. Your job is to shoot the can off the log. Emboldened by the feel of the cold steel in your hands, you raise the storied weapon to your shoulder, take careful aim as well as you can considering you can't see the target, and gently, confidently, you shoot. And you miss.

That's called a shot in the dark...and that is exactly what we do when we respond to an RFP that we get "out of the blue." We might get lucky every once in a while, but often as not, we're just wasting resources responding to something we're never, or hardly ever, going to win.

There are two "shot in the dark" ratios we're going to calculate, the shot in the dark proposal response ratio and the shot in the dark proposal win ratio.

Shot in the dark proposal response ratio

The shot in the dark proposal response ratio gives insight into how often you chase RFPs where your potential of winning is really, really low. It is calculated by dividing the number of RFPs you actually knew about at least six months before the RFP was issued, divided by the number of RFPs you respond to.

Shot in the dark proposal win ratio

The Shot in the dark proposal win ratio further clarifies the futility of responding to RFPs you receive out of the blue. It is similar to the response ratio, but it's focused on how often you actually win a contract when the RFP that prompted it was received "out of the blue." It is calculated by dividing the number of RFPs you knew about at least six months before the RFP was issued, divided by the number you ultimately won.

The purpose of these shot in the dark ratios is to raise awareness among managers about how effectively they are using their resources and, in particular, if resources are being wasted pursuing opportunities when there's no realistic chance at winning.

OTHER WAYS TO CALCULATE WIN RATIOS

Calculating win ratios is a great way to gain insight into the effectiveness of your proposal effort, but you gain even more insight by adding more dimensions to the performance data you collect. Specifically, you can view win rates at a more granular level by calculating them at a market or division level. You can also calculate win rates by including revenue in addition to number of opportunities.

Segregating ratios by market or division

Many companies that offer an array of products or services will organize their sales efforts according to some criteria. It could be line of business, target market, geographic territory, etc.

Depending on the complexity of your organization and the volume of proposals you produce, it might make sense to go one step further and calculate each of the eight win ratios for each of the organizational units you've defined. For example, a technology company may have two divisions; one that targets government and another that targets commercial markets. Instead of calculating win ratios for the entire organization, this firm might gain far more insight into their proposal effectiveness by calculating separate win ratios for each market.

Adding revenue as another dimension

Suppose you respond to ten RFPs, and only win one. Your win rate is 10%. But also suppose the nine RFP opportunities you lost were each worth $10,000 while the one you won was worth $1,000,000. That makes a difference.

I prefer tracking win rates by opportunity. This gives you the best overall view of your business development efforts. But adding revenue into the calculation adds another dimension that makes the information you collect more meaningful.

CHAPTER RECAP

If you're serious about getting better, about improving your win rate or reducing your losses, you should understand, embrace, and then implement the best practices articulated in this chapter.

- Best practice #1: Do an internal "lessons learned" review
- Best practice #2: Request and analyze copies of competitive proposals
- Best practice #3: Perform answer-by-answer comparisons
- Best practice #4: Perform post-decision interviews with buyers
- Best practice #5: Develop metrics to track your performance

11. To Protest or Not to Protest?

Before you draw any conclusions or take any actions, please read the entire chapter and try to understand the fundamental meaning, the underlying message. This chapter is not legal advice, it's not even a recommendation; it's a slightly tongue-in-cheek effort to refocus you, the seller, on the unfortunate fact that some buyers do not want to work with you. You can try to make them, but it's always best if they want to work with you (hint, hint—that's the underlying message).

If you want to protest after reading this, go for it. But if you do, consider seeking the services of an attorney experienced in this area.

Don't protest. You may now proceed to the next chapter.

…awkward silence…

"Wait a minute, Dave," you may object, after enduring the awkward silence. "But isn't that a rather broad stroke of the veto pen? You've been so informational and educational throughout this book until now. Can you offer a bit more of an explanation about why we shouldn't protest?"

"Sure," says I. "You can protest, if you want. Go ahead. Knock yourself out. But if you do, you're likely going to lose."

"Wow. You sound really sure of yourself, Dave, sure that we're going to lose if we protest. Why is that?"

"Because," I respond, "if they really wanted to hire you, they would have."

"You're sure."

"Yup."

...more awkward silence...

"But what if we find out there were some inappropriate shenanigans surrounding the decision process? For example, what if we learn one of the vendors should have been disqualified for some reason but won anyway? Isn't that a good reason to protest?"

"Nope," says I.

"Why not?"

"Because," I repeat, "if they really wanted to hire you, they would have. But they didn't, did they? They wanted another vendor. The vendor they wanted is the vendor that won."

...still more of that painful, awkward silence...

"But what if it's something simple like they added up the points incorrectly?," you ask. "Isn't that a good reason to protest?"

"Nope," says I. "That's a good reason to call your contact and explain the mathematical error. Then, if it really was an error, if they really want to work with your company, they're going to issue a great big mea culpa, they're going to recalculate the points, and you're going to win. No protest necessary."

...another awkward and now somewhat strained silence...

"But what if..." you begin, before I rudely interrupt.

"Look," I say, in an effort to cut to the bottom line, "it's like this. People who understand the procurement process recognize it isn't always as fair and objective as many procurement people promote it to be and many sellers wish it to be. You might have the greatest solution, the best proposal, and the lowest cost, but if the buyer has already decided they're buying from ABC company, then they're going to buy from ABC company. They win, you lose, and there's virtually nothing you can do about it.

"Sure, you could protest, but even if you're successful in having the procurement reconsidered or rebid, they're still going to find a way to choose the vendor they wanted all along. In fact, I've only encountered a few times, in my entire career, where a protest was ultimately successful in winning business for the protester."

"But, hey," you say, "if we win because of the protest, that's a good thing, right?"

"Nope," I respond. "Not even close. See, the buyer wanted to work with ABC company, but because of your successful protest, now they're forced to work with you, instead. They don't want to, but they have to. Now, you tell me, how well do you think that relationship is going to work? Is this client going to be happy? Is this contract going to be profitable? Or are the next three years of the contract going to rank among the most miserable 36 months of your professional career?

"One more thing," I continue. "When you protest, you run the risk of getting a reputation as a protester. And while this will not necessarily prevent you from being included in future procurements and awards, there's a possibility it might. Procurement people don't like protests. It reflects negatively on them. So if they can find a way to exclude you from future procurements or future awards, it's possible they might.

"See my point? Just because you win doesn't mean you've won. If they wanted to work with you, they would have chosen you. But they didn't. And if you use the system to make them work with you when they really want to work with someone else, they're not going to like it and it's not going to make them like you. In fact, they're likely going to resent it. There's going to be tension and animosity, and all of it is going to be directed at you and your team."

"So what should I do?" you ask.

"Well, first off, don't protest. Don't ever try to MAKE them work with you, it's best if they WANT to work with you. So if you lose, accept it, as bitter as it may be. But then, before the next procurement, do all of the other things you need to do to build relationships, establish your credibility, and in general, get them to WANT to work with you. If you do these things, you're going to win a lot more business than if you go around protesting every time you do not win.

"If you're still really upset about the outcome or the way it was handled, take some time and rant to your associates. Sound out why you're upset and give yourself a chance to vent some steam. I say this because, sometimes, often times, people protest more because they're mad at losing than because they believe they have a legitimate claim.

"If you're still upset after that, consider calling the buyer contact to express your concerns. Explain what happened, and why you think the procurement was unfair. Don't use the "P" word, but calmly express what led you to this point. See what he or she says."

Then, if you still want to file a protest, ignore my advice and file a protest. Don't worry, I'll be OK.

HERE'S THE BOTTOM LINE—*READ THIS*

Remember back at the beginning of the book where we discussed how different people have different views of best practices? Remember where I encouraged you to ask, *best practices according to whom*? This is one of those times where you should ask, *best practices according to whom*?

I offer this admonition because, on the topic of protests, I'm in the minority.

I'm in the minority

There are many veteran proposal experts who disagree with my views on protesting. They advocate that sellers should be ready to protest whenever there's even a whiff of shenanigans or inappropriate behavior. One of them is my friend, Dr. David Nealey, of WordSmart Business Services.

David argues if a seller invests tens or hundreds of thousands of dollars building a solution and drafting a proposal, it's hard not to protest if there are signs of funny business, skullduggery, rules not being followed, or other kinds of unethical behavior. He went further, saying it's almost an obligation to protest, when appropriate, because it keeps buyers honest knowing sellers will push back if the buyers don't follow the rules.

The point is there are many proposal professionals, like David, who will tell you the best practice is to protest if an error was made, rules weren't followed, something was amiss, etc. To David, and others who share his view, protesting is a best practice when used appropriately and wisely.

This is why you have to ask, "best practice according to whom?" And then you have to make up your own mind about which of us you agree with.

So what's the answer?

I've made the case against protesting because I'd rather work with someone who actually wants to work with me than someone who's forced to work with me. I believe it will result in better outcomes. But ultimately, you'll have to make that decision for yourself based on what you think is in the best interest of your company. That's a decision only you and your team can make.

Consider getting an attorney

There are some attorneys who specialize in handling protests for federal or state and local government bids. If you decide to protest, consider hiring one of these specialists. They know the law, of course, but they also know the politics. They can guide you through the process, counsel you when not to protest, help you avoid the hazards, and in general, improve your chances for a favorable outcome.

CHAPTER RECAP

Don't protest. Or protest if you want to. It's totally up to you. If you do protest, though, consider talking with an attorney.

Part 3: Business Development and Sales Messaging Best Practices

12. Summarizing the RFP Selling Process

The RFP Selling process is a continuum of tasks that span up to 36 months—24 months before the RFP is issued, and as many as 12 months after your proposal is submitted. It begins with pre-RFP selling, continues through the kickoff meeting and proposal development phase, and in cases where you are shortlisted—where you advance to the next step in the selection process—includes the post-submission sales presentation.

The rest of this chapter *summarizes* the RFP selling process, and in particular, each of these major phases related to business development and messaging. The chapters immediately following this chapter explore each topic in greater depth.

1. PRE-RFP SELLING: MAKING THE SALE AND DOCUMENTING THE OPPORTUNITY

This phase of the RFP selling process has two important functions. The first is to make the sale.

In chapter 2, we discussed the importance of being proactive instead of reactive, of meeting with buyers and "making the sale" in the 12 to 24 months before the RFP is issued. If you don't make the sale before the RFP comes out, your chances of winning are low. Really low. Single digits low.

The second function of this phase is to capture as much intelligence information as possible about the decision makers, the influencers, their individual motivations and perceptions of risk, the process they will use to make their purchase decision, etc.

These are just a few of the many things you need to know in order to write a customer-focused proposal; there are many more. The point is it's important you identify these things in the months and years before the RFP is issued so you're ready once it's released.

2. KICKOFF MEETINGS AND PROPOSAL DEVELOPMENT PLANNING

Once the RFP comes out, it's time to schedule a kickoff meeting.

In most organizations today, proposal kickoff meetings are too administrative. They're focused more on assigning tasks and establishing deadlines than figuring out how you're going to make the sale. This needs to change.

If you want to win more of the RFPs you pursue, you need to expand the scope of your kickoff meetings to include a sales strategy component. In other words, you need to treat your proposal development projects more like sales opportunities to win instead of writing projects to complete.

The sales strategy component of your kickoff meeting should address these four critical tasks:

1. Scrutinizing the RFP
2. Organizing and analyzing what you know
3. Configuring your solution
4. Configuring your sales message

Pre-Kickoff meeting: scrutinizing the RFP

The first step after receiving an RFP, and before the first kickoff meeting takes place, is to scrutinize the RFP. Almost everyone reads an RFP, but not everyone analyzes an RFP. Not everyone scrutinizes an RFP to uncover gems of information that might otherwise be hidden in its pages. This is what I propose you begin doing.

Before the first kickoff meeting begins, a few key people on your business development and proposal team need to scrutinize the RFP to learn as much as you can about the opportunity. This includes things like reviewing the general description the buyer provides and then reconciling that against how they award points. It includes things like identifying content you expected that isn't included, and content you didn't expect that is included. It includes things like identifying questions or requirements that appear to be written by a competitor. See the point? You aren't just reading it, you're scrutinizing it.

By employing this careful, meticulous approach, you will likely find things you weren't aware of prior, and that's a good thing. It's good because the more you know and the more informed you are, the better and more responsive your proposal will be.

Kickoff meeting part 1: Compiling, organizing, and analyzing what you know

Your salespeople have so far done a good job selling to the decision makers and collecting information about the buyer before the RFP was issued, and you've invested time scrutinizing your RFP to find everything else. Well done.

The next big job is to compile, organize, and analyze all of the information you've collected. Compiling and organizing the information is fairly straight forward. More challenging is analyzing the information you've collected to figure out what it all means.

Analyzing the information requires pulling together your entire team to discuss, perhaps argue, but ultimately agree on the major issues the customer faces and you have to address. The analysis part of the meeting is accomplished by asking and then answering a series of questions such as, "What is their primary issue, objective, or outcome?" "What obstacles will we have to overcome and how are we going to do it?"

By its conclusion, everyone who participates in this meeting will understand the buyer's challenges and objectives, and by extension, what you are going to have to address if you have any hope of making a sale.

Kickoff meeting part 2: Configuring your solution

Too many people use the word solution as a synonym for a product or service. It's not.

A solution is assembled from multiple components. One of those components is your product or service, of course, but there are others.

For example, your solution may include payroll processing services, but the actual solution you configure may also include two months of onsite service to ease the transition from the buyer's existing payroll provider, quarterly briefings about changes in state and federal payroll rules and requirements, handholding-level support for the buyer's remote office in Duluth, etc.

The point is you are not selling a product or a service, you are selling a unique solution to their unique problem or issue. It's built around your service, sure, but it's uniquely tailored to them and their needs.

Only after you identify your solution can you even begin to figure out what your message should be.

Kickoff meeting part 3: Configuring your sales message

Now that you've configured your solution, the last major task of your kickoff meeting should be to configure your sales message. Indeed, everybody who is going to be involved in writing or reviewing content should have a shared understanding of the message your proposal should articulate. This way it will sound like a cohesive document written by a single person or a coordinated team of people rather than a disjointed cacophony of ideas written by multiple writers who don't know or can't agree on what their message should be.

3. CREATING POST-SUBMISSION SALES PRESENTATIONS

Some organizations have a multi-step buying process; after reviewing all of the proposals they receive, they choose three finalists who are then invited onsite to deliver a presentation to decision makers. This is often called "making it to the short list." Following these onsite presentations, the buyer then chooses their preferred vendor.

The entire business development team—including proposal managers, writers, and SMEs—should be a part of creating this presentation. It should follow from, and be built around, the proposal that got you to this point.

The major topics summarized in this chapter are discussed in more detail in the following six chapters.

CHAPTER RECAP

The RFP selling process, done correctly, takes as much as 36 months—up to 24 months before the RFP is issued, and as many as 12 months after your proposal is submitted. It has three main phases:

1. Pre-RFP selling and discovery
2. Kickoff meetings and proposal development
3. Post-submission sales presentations

It's time consuming, to be sure, but if you do it well, you will increase your win rate.

13. Pre-RFP Selling and Discovery: Documenting the Opportunity

This chapter explores the first phase of the RFP selling process—pre-RFP selling and discovery. This is where the true selling work begins. It's where your salespeople meet with decision makers and influencers, get to know them, build trust, educate them about you and your business, identify the challenges they face, uncover opportunities for improvement, establish your team's credibility, suggest solutions to their problems, and do all the other things that salespeople should do to win an opportunity. In short, it's where you make the sale.

Within the context of a formal procurement, though, this is also where your salespeople—or your operations staff if you currently manage the contract—collect as much information as they can about the buyer, the program, its history, and more. The more you know before the RFP is released, the better off you'll be as you transition into the proposal development phase of the effort.

DOCUMENT THE PROGRAM OR PROJECT

The first step in your information gathering efforts involves understanding the program they're putting out to bid. This includes understanding their current program as it exists today, what they want in a new program, how their program has evolved over time, etc.

Current program

If this is a current program, one that is already in place and is periodically rebid every few years, begin by documenting what the program looks like today. It may be difficult to get all of this information, but here's a good framework:

- Have they given their current program a name? If not, how do they refer to it internally?
- Describe the program in as much detail as you can. Use the approach journalists employ; ask who, what, where, when, why, and how?
- Document how many of their internal staff interact with the program on a fulltime or part-time basis? Which roles are they?
- If you can, figure out their current budget for the program.

Your goals are to develop a thorough understanding of the program and get as much detail as you can.

What they want in the new program

It is important to document any changes from the buyer's current program to the new program they're going to be seeking with the new RFP. Whenever you find an important change, it suggests they want something they aren't currently getting. It might also suggest their needs have changed so they need something additional. Your job is to figure out what that something is. Consider these examples.

- If a hospital is already working with a staffing vendor to provide nurses, I'd be highly intrigued to learn the next RFP will include a condition that they don't have to pay if a nurse leaves the position within three months. Why are they including this condition? Is this a problem today?
- If the buyer already gets reports, but wants to completely revamp their reporting package, I want to know why. Are they not getting what they want today? Has a new person been hired who is more sophisticated in his approach to data analysis?

As a salesperson confronted with either of these examples, I'd want to learn more. They're obviously issues the customer currently cares about.

If I uncover and understand those things in more depth, I could both build a better solution and write more effective content to address their concerns and fulfill their requirements.

Changes over time

When learning about a buyer's program, you should always try to understand its evolution. This offers insight into the program that might help you leverage things that are important to them, and avoid things they've already tried that didn't work.

To use the hospital staffing example, suppose they initially did all of their recruiting using internal resources, but when good nurses became harder to find, they realized they needed outside help. They hired a large, national staffing firm that looked great on paper, but didn't have many resources or connections within their local community. Then they hired a small, local recruiting company that performed better because they were well connected locally, but lacked the size and depth that was needed as the hospital continued to grow.

Understanding this background won't necessarily help you win the next bid. On the other hand, it might help you build a narrative that acknowledges the challenges of finding a staffing firm that is both large enough to satisfy their program demands *and* well-connected within the local nursing community. Most veteran proposal writers could do a good job selling that idea, but not unless they first understood this background and the various iterations leading up to today.

Specific grievances and/or opportunities

When investigating a buyer's program, always keep your ears open for any sign, mention, or suggestion that a buyer is either unhappy or wants something more than they're currently getting. Here are some examples.

I was working with a staffing vendor during the pre-RFP discovery phase of their selling effort when we learned that the buyer's accounting staff was frustrated with their current vendor. We learned the vendor's invoices were often incorrect, and when the staff accountant responsible for reconciling invoices asked questions, the vendor took forever to provide answers. Even then, the answers were vague and not always actionable.

After learning this, we arranged to have one of our accounting managers meet with their staff accountant to learn more about her challenges and how she wanted the process to work. The two began a professional and then a friendly relationship that turned into an advantage for us.

I love this example because, clearly, the way you invoice your client has little to do with the primary service you provide. It's incidental. From the buyer's perspective, though, it's not incidental, it's a fundamental part of the total user experience. If you provide a great service, but your invoicing function is flawed, that's frustrating for the buyer, potentially creates more work for them, and if it's bad enough, opens the door to another provider.

This is precisely why salespeople should always work to identify the buyer's grievances or frustrations with their current program and vendor. It's only after identifying them that you can exploit them in your proposed solution.

IDENTIFY AND EVALUATE THE CURRENT VENDOR

Before the RFP is issued, sellers must learn who the current vendor is, how well they're managing the current program, and how they're perceived by the various decision makers within the buying organization.

What is the vendor's standing with the buyer?

After identifying the current vendor, it's important to poll the relevant decision makers and influencers to discover how the vendor is perceived. Do the decision makers like the vendor? Are they frustrated? Is it a mix?

Understanding these general perceptions is important, but it's even better to dig into the details. If a decision maker is frustrated by the current vendor, you need to discover the source of their frustration. If Sally is frustrated with Vendor A, that's good to know. If Sally is frustrated because she can't get anyone on their support staff to return phone calls, that's much better because it's the kind of actionable intelligence you can use in your proposal response.

The more you know, the better you'll be able to position yourself as a favorable alternative when you write your proposal.

Does the current vendor offer some value-added service the buyer would lose if they changed vendors?

Sometimes, a vendor will offer a value-added service that is tangential to their primary service, but it's something buyers find highly valuable. So while they may perceive your primary service to be more of a commodity, they shudder at the thought of losing the value-added service you offer.

- One contractor I worked with managed a large program for a state government. The buyer wasn't particularly enamored with the contractor, but they loved the contractor's employee who managed the program. She was competent, able, she forgot more about the industry than most people knew, she had lots of important contacts at the state level (it was a state contract), and she had a positive personality everyone liked. They were willing to replace the contractor, but not this program manager.

- Another vendor I worked with was a small company with great service. But they also had a contract with an industry veteran who was available to offer insight and guidance not only to the firm but to its clients. Their clients valued her guidance. It was additional value that the buyer received and did not want to lose.

These are only two examples, but they reflect the bigger issue. If your competitor provides one or more value-added services, and you hope to win the contract away from them, you will probably have to find a way to replicate the value the other vendor is currently providing. At the very least, you have to identify what the buyer is going to lose if they replace their current vendor with you. If you can account for it, if you can minimize their loss, you've just increased your chances.

Explore the incumbent vendor's website

When another company is the incumbent vendor, it's important to spend at least some time analyzing their website. Sometimes, you learn nothing. Other times, it's amazing what you can learn.

First, do a general review to see how they present themselves specific to the product or service you're selling.

- Try to get a general sense for their corporate culture. Are they young, energetic, and innovative? Are they mature and established? Something in between?
- Determine their organizational focus. Are they your direct competitor? Or are they mainly focused in other areas and where you compete with them is just one small part of their operations?

Second, look for any references to the buyer you are pursuing. Has the vendor written press releases about that company? Have they documented any case studies or user stories or chooser stories about why the buyer is working with them or chose them? If so, who do they quote and how recent were those stories? I'd be particularly interested in any user story that centers around Sally, for example, since she's no longer there. And if the story is from four or five years ago, but nothing more recent, I'd be interested in that, too. Consequently, if a decision maker at the buyer's organization recently agreed to be a reference in a user story, that's also relevant.

Sometimes, often times, you learn nothing from these reviews. Other times, though, you find gold. You never know until you look.

IF WE ARE THE INCUMBENT, WHERE DO WE STAND?

One of the biggest mistakes that many sellers make when bidding on incumbent contracts is they act entitled. They act arrogant. They act like, "we're already doing this job well, so just choose us and we'll continuing doing the job well without any interruptions to service."

Buyers _hate it_ when sellers do this. They're thinking to themselves, "All of the other vendors competing for the procurement are taking it seriously, why aren't you? All of the other vendors are trying to sell new and innovative ways they can provide better service than you do, and do it at competitive prices or even lower prices than you offer, why aren't you?" If you assume the business is yours, or they get the tiniest notion you think you're entitled just because you're the incumbent, you're in troubled waters.

> Even when you are the incumbent, you have to approach the opportunity like you are a competitor trying to unseat the incumbent.

You are in a position of knowledge because you've been working with their staff for the last two and a half years, but that doesn't generally mean you're a shoe in. It means you know a lot more than any of your competitors about the people making the decisions, and what they want professionally and personally. You have insights. But that doesn't ensure you will win. Nor should it.

What you should be doing at this point is evaluating where you stand with this buyer. Call your program staff into a meeting and find out as much as you can. Ask your staff questions like these:

- What is the customer's general view of our company?
- What do they like about us?
- What do they dislike about us? Can we fix it?
- What are our vulnerabilities? Can we fix them?
- Are there any opportunities we can build on?
- What about the individuals...Bob was our biggest champion but his influence in the organization has waned. Who is our champion now?
- Jane was the internal program manager and she liked us, but she moved to a new division. Sally is the new program manager. Do we know where she stands?
- Have we collected any glowing accolades—favorable emails, attaboys, or awards—over the previous couple years we could reference in this proposal?

GET TO KNOW THE DECISION MAKERS

This section is all about identifying the people—the decision makers and influencers—who are involved in making purchase decisions. It's about learning who they are, their roles, their influence within the organization, their personal motivations, and more.

Titles and roles

There's a difference between titles and roles. I make this point because, as a junior salesperson, I was always taught to find the senior manager within the organization who has the decision making authority. As a veteran salesperson, though, I now know this approach can put me in contact with the wrong person.

Within the world of formal procurements, and especially within those procurements where decisions are made by review committees, someone's title is often less important than their role. For example, I was once involved in a procurement (on the buying side) where a mid-level staff member was in charge of the selection. We picked him to lead the effort because he was the de facto authority on the service we were buying. He knew more than the rest of us, and he led the rest of us. Salespeople taught to seek out the highest ranking decision maker flocked around the president of our company, who was also on the committee. The smart salespeople, in contrast, figured out it was this mid-level staffer who was leading the effort and focused most of their selling efforts around him. In this procurement, that's where the power was, and that's who led the rest of us to the decision that he wanted us to make. The point is purchase decisions aren't always made by the person with the most senior title.

In procurements for state and local governments and educational institutions, building consensus is often highly valued. Therefore, many of the people involved in the selection process are from positions throughout the organization. Understanding their titles and roles, and the departments where they work, will help you to better understand the makeup of the selection body so you can more effectively target your sales message to these decision makers.

Vendor preferences

If a buying organization chooses a vendor, it's fairly safe to assume that not everybody within their organization agrees with that choice. Some may have preferred another vendor, instead.

As your salespeople are networking throughout the organization and identifying decision makers and building relationships and doing all of those sales things, they should also be identifying each person's vendor preferences. Perhaps a particular decision maker thinks your company is the best vendor. Good for you! Pat yourself on your back. But make sure you understand *why* they think this. Maybe another decision maker thinks another company is the best vendor for the job. Not good for you, perhaps, but not necessarily the end of the world, either. Find out why they like the other vendor. Are they firm in their convictions? Or are they open to considering alternatives?

The more you know about each decision maker's views, the more effective you'll be able to craft proposal content that sways their opinions.

Personal motivations

This is a big one.

Personal motivations drive organizational requirements. We discussed motivations at length in chapter 5. We discussed the importance of selling to people, not organizations.

Understanding a decision maker's motivations is necessary if you are going to write compelling, customer-focused content. The more you know, the more effective your writing will be.

Name	Title	Driving Motivation
Julie Jones	Controller	Personally responsible for fixing all of the errors resulting from manual input of payroll records, and she hates being hated when she has to recover cash from employees who are overpaid. Wants a better system to input all of their different kinds of payroll records without

		having to rekey everything manually.
Hank Smith	Payroll clerk	Hates getting blamed for all of the errors from rekeying all payroll records into the current vendor's manual system. Wants a smoother, more automated process that reduces errors.
Jane Peters	HR Director	Has talked with some hourly employees who live paycheck to paycheck, and can't afford to have a checking account. She learned these employees have to pay fees to cash their checks. She doesn't like that. For these folks, she wants pay to be distributed by debit cards so they can access all of their pay without having to pay any check cashing fees.

The more effectively you can identify the personal motivations of the people making the decisions, the more effectively you'll be able to target your content to what they care about the most.

Personal perceptions of risk

Risk is a kind of motivation, so technically, it should be covered in the previous section. I present it separately because risk is so important; *nothing will kill a sale faster than if a buyer perceives too much risk.*

Notice I use the word, *perceive*. Remember that risk is not a fact, it's a perception, and different people have different perceptions. This necessarily means that in any given situation, it's not what you know to be true, it's what they perceive to be true.

Also notice I use the phrase, *too much risk*. In any sales transaction, there is always some risk. The buyer is trying to evaluate how much risk there is.

> Nothing else you say is relevant if the buyer perceives your product, solution, or company as being too risky.

This is why it's so important for your salespeople and business development people to meet and get to know all of the buyers involved in the procurement long before the RFP comes out. If you can figure out what their motivations are, and in particular their perceptions of risk, you'll be in a much better position to address them and give your company a legitimate shot at winning the business.

Record your notes into a table, much like we did for motivations.

Name	Title	Perception of Risk
Julie Jones	Controller	She has acknowledged that our solution is a good fit with their needs, but she is concerned about the disruption moving from one vendor to another. She's got other projects going on, and a big audit coming up. She's worried the time and effort to switch vendors might be more than they can handle.
Hank Smith	Payroll clerk	Hank doesn't like our sales guy, Bob. In fact, he told Julie that he thinks Bob will say whatever he has to in order to get the business. That's got him questioning everything Bob has proposed. Also, Hank isn't looking forward to working with Bob regularly if we get the business.

These two examples are fictional, but they aren't made up. They're based on real life situations. Despite this, they are perfect examples of the kinds of risk people perceive.

Identify the various buying influences, and their personal objectives and motivations

So far, we've talked a lot about the decision makers, but we should also be thinking about the "influencers," the people who may not have buying authority but still influence the buying decision.

Many years ago, I was a young sales guy, a total rookie, selling software tools mostly to small city and regional government departments. I was trying hard to close a sale for a report writer software package. I had the right guy, he was the department manager with decision-making authority and a budget—all things salespeople are taught to look for. I also learned he didn't like the tool they had been using. Over the course of a few sales calls, he agreed we had the tool he needed, and that it was better than what they were currently using.

"OK, I'm sold," he said at the end of one call.

"Great, I'll send you a contract," I replied quickly.

"Not so fast, Dave," he said. My heart sunk. "The last time I bought a new tool without my team knowing about it, they gave me grief for a month. I like the tool and I think we need it, but now you have to convince them. If they're on board, so am I. If they say no, I say no."

I had the right guy, a manager with decision-making authority AND the budget to spend—just like they taught me to do in all those sales classes I attended. Despite that, I never accounted for the significant role that the influencers would play in the decision-making process. In this case, their opinions were just as important as the manager's decision.

With a few more years of selling under my belt, I now understand an influencer's role can vary dramatically by organization, their commitment to building consensus, and the strength of the personalities involved. However it works, you must be aware of the people who influence buying decisions.

Who are the champions and the antagonists?

There are generally two types of buyers—be they decision makers or influencers—that I always want to know well. They are the champions and the antagonists.

IDENTIFY YOUR CHAMPION

The champions want us to win. For whatever reason—maybe she knew us from a previous company, for example, or our sales message is exactly what she is looking for—champions likes us and want to see us win the procurement. They may even help us by coaching us who to talk with in the organization, what messages we should be stressing, etc.

We need to identify these people, and we absolutely must understand why they like us and what they want. The better we understand what they want, the more effectively we can help them get what they want and the stronger will be their resolve to help us win.

IDENTIFY THE ANTAGONISTS

Just like every good story has its protagonists, it's champions, it also has it antagonists. In the proposal world, the antagonists are champions for another vendor.

Antagonists are not bad people and you should not think of them that way. They generally don't hate you. It's just they are champions for another vendor like other buyers are champions for you.

It's hard to win these people over to your side, but it's good to at least learn who they are. If you can, it's even better to get to know them. Find out why they like the other vendor or, if they don't like you, *why* they don't like you. If you can somehow defuse some of their dislike for you, they may not favor you, but they may not be aggressively against you, either.

With enough information and understanding, you might be able to mitigate their argument by including content in your proposal that addresses and maybe defuses the relevant issues or concerns they cite.

Research the decision makers

Salespeople should always research the decision makers and influencers involved in the procurement…*within reason*. This means you should look them up on LinkedIn,™ or Facebook,™ or any other social media or news source that is in the public domain. You should probably stop short of hiring a private investigator. That'd be kinda creepy.

When I investigate decision makers, I'm looking for things that will give me insight into their thinking:

- What professional organizations do they belong to, how long have they been involved, and what role do they play?
- What schools have they gone to, and what did they study?
- How long have they been in their current job?
- What jobs were they in before this one, and what companies did they work for before this company?

- On LinkedIn.com especially, I try to identify the discussion groups they participate in. If I can, I read some of their posts. These offer insights into their views.
- Also on LinkedIn.com, I look to see what recommendations they've given or received, and what organizations they follow.

Sometimes, what you learn doesn't help except for general background information. Other times, you learn something that can be very helpful. Just recently, for example, we encountered a buyer who was relatively new in his position, and because of our research, we learned he had almost no relevant experience prior to taking his current job. He was an inexperienced rookie who was thrust into a management role for a job he knew little about. Since we had a veteran of that industry on staff, we emphasized in our messaging that if he chose our service, he would also have access to our people and their expertise. It was more subtle, but the essence of our message was this:

> *We know you're new in this position, and don't have a lot of experience, so you're probably feeling a little bit underwater. Our service is going to do everything we said it would. You're going to look like a hero for selecting us.*

> *But even more, by working with us, you have access to experienced industry veterans. These people are experts. They've forgotten more than most people know. If you are working with us, these experts are available to you to offer guidance, answer questions, help you understand challenges and formulate decisions, and more.*

See the point? The more you know about the people you're selling to, the more effectively you'll be able to target your message to what they care about most.

DOCUMENT THE CIRCUMSTANCES

When I first get an RFP, I have all kinds of questions, and not all of them are related to what we're selling or what the customer is buying. I want to know about the circumstances surrounding the opportunity, and

I always begin with this question: "Why did the buyer publish this RFP *now?*"

Why are they going to bid now?

Essentially, organizations go out to bid for one of two reasons; because they have to or because they want to. As sellers, we need to know which it is.

Going out to bid because they have to

In general, most state and local government organizations, and many large or midsize commercial organizations, are *required*—by law, regulation, or internal company rules—to go out to bid about every three to five years. In other words, the real buyers in the organization, the internal people responsible for managing a particular program, have little or no choice in the matter. It's forced upon them.

Recognize the significance of this. It means at least some and perhaps many RFPs are issued as a result of some arbitrary requirement, not because the decision maker is seriously considering changing vendors.

Consider the case of a program manager who is completely happy with her current vendor. Further, suppose she's so busy with other projects and day-to-day responsibilities she hardly has enough time to get lunch much less endure the arduous process of replacing a vendor. Despite all that, her company issues an RFP because her procurement department is making her do it.

As a competitive vendor bidding on the contract, what are your realistic chances of replacing the current vendor? I'm not much of a betting man, but I'd wager your chances are pretty low.

Going out to bid because they want to

The other reason a buying organization goes out to bid is because they want to. The fact that someone *wants* to go out to bid is itself relevant—it tells us they're motivated by something.

Let's start with this fundamental truth: most program managers don't like going out to bid. Going out to bid is time consuming and tedious. It requires they do a lot of research and information collecting, write an

RFP, organize a team of people who are resistant because they're already busy with other work, get bombarded by vendor salespeople trying to get last minute insights, review a bunch of proposals that are longwinded and generally boring, etc. Even worse, a lot of procurement people start hanging around telling them what they are and are not allowed to do during the course of the procurement.

On top of all that, there's the R word—*Risk*. Program managers don't like risk. Imagine going through a big procurement process, selecting a new vendor, and only then discovering the vendor you just chose is nowhere near as good as the vendor you just had.

So now, despite all of the difficulties they will endure, despite all the hassle they're going to face, despite the inherent risk they will incur, *they still want to go out to bid*!?!? Are they crazy? Do they enjoy punishment?

Or maybe, just maybe, is there some other reason? Hmmm.

Specific circumstances

When faced with a buyer that *wants* to go out to bid, the next logical question becomes, "Why? Why do they want to go out to bid now?" That's a good question. Indeed, that's the pivotal question.

In general, there are five major reasons that buyers want to go out to bid. Understanding which one you're dealing with is critical to making good decisions about how you're going to respond.

1. Management change

When I am the competition selling against an incumbent, a change in management is one of my favorite scenarios. That's because when a new manager comes in, he or she frequently wants to "change things up." When this happens, it is often a threat to the incumbent, but it opens the door to the competition. Good for you if you're the competition, not so much if you're the incumbent.

Be wary, though. Sometimes the new manager simply wants to bring in the same vendor he was using at his previous company. As a veteran proposal writer, I've been on both sides of this issue; I've won new business when a manager who likes us moved to a new company and brought us in there, but I've also lost business when a new manager took over a program where we were the incumbent and replaced us with the vendor they preferred.

Just be aware—and wary—if an RFP is related to a management change. It has implications, and they aren't always clear. You need to figure out what those implications are.

2. Significant change to program requirements

It's difficult or sometimes even contractually impossible to ask an existing vendor to significantly change their program in the middle of a contract. So when a program's requirements change significantly, buyers will often issue a new RFP.

This is an opportunity for competing vendors because, in a sense, there is no incumbent vendor for the newly published specifications. The existing vendor still has an advantage, but the door has been opened a crack.

Incidentally, this is one of the reasons why you should always keep a copy of past RFPs. You can learn a lot by comparing the new RFP to the previous RFP to see what's changed from then to now. This comparison can shed great insight into their thinking and maybe even their motivations.

3. Economic conditions change

After the so-called Great Recession began in 2008, many buyers issued new RFPs—sometimes before the existing contract term ended—because there was internal pressure to cut costs. When a buyer goes to bid early for this reason, it's an opportunity for competitive firms, *but only if they're willing and able to get aggressive on pricing*.

I want to reiterate that last point. Some salespeople will stubbornly sell value no matter what. But if money is so tight that a buyer goes out to bid early, you cannot promote value and win. The successful bidder is the one who embraces the lost cost message and provides the lowest cost solution. In this scenario, if a low cost approach is not something you can offer, or if you only want to compete on value and not cost, *don't bid*.

4. Current vendor is falling short

If you learn that a buyer is going out to bid because they are dissatisfied with their current contractor, you've got a legitimate opportunity. It's not definite they're going to change from their current vendor; they may just be using the RFP as a way to shake up the vendor or get some new performance guarantees. Still, the buyer is at least open to a new vendor that has a good story to tell.

This scenario is one of your best chances to unseat an incumbent vendor. If you're going to invest resources into any opportunity, this is probably one of the best.

5. To squeeze the current vendor for a better deal

Sometimes, buyers will go out to bid with no intention of changing vendors, they just want to negotiate a better deal with their current vendor. There's no better way to conduct a negotiation than when it's accompanied by competitive pressure, so they use your organization for no other reason than to put pressure on their current vendor and improve their negotiating position.

The program manager is still going out to bid because they want to, not because they have to, but this scenario isn't good for a competing vendor trying to unseat the incumbent.

When your organization is put in this position, you're sometimes referred to as "column fodder." When a buyer is likely going to stay with the incumbent vendor, but the procurement staff wants the procurement to at least appear to be competitive, they reach out to competing sellers and invite them to bid even though these sellers aren't legitimately in the running. You don't have a chance at winning but you're still serving a purpose for the procurement officer; you're filling up a column so they can say the procurement is competitive. In other words, you're column fodder.

Why any of this matters

What's important to take away from this discussion is that you have to understand the circumstances surrounding the release of an RFP. If a so-called buyer goes out to bid because he has to, not because he wants to, what's the likelihood he's going to switch vendors? If he goes out to bid because he's not happy with his current vendor, in contrast, the odds go up in your favor.

Every scenario is different, and if you have any hope of making a sale, you have to understand it.

DOCUMENT THE DECISION MODEL AND CRITERIA

Buyers use a variety of decision criteria and models to evaluate the proposals they receive and, ultimately, to choose a vendor. During the pre-RFP discovery phase, it's important you identify both the criteria and the model they're using.

Documenting decision models

The model an organization uses is generally dictated by procurement policy within commercial or private organizations, by laws or regulations within state and local government agencies, and by laws or regulations in publicly-financed educational organizations.

For publicly-funded educational institutions or state and local government agencies, you will typically encounter either these or some variation of these models:

- Proposals are reviewed by contracting officers to identify those that meet minimum RFP requirements. Of these, the proposal that offers the lowest price wins.
- Proposals are reviewed by contracting officers to identify those that meet minimum RFP requirements. Of these, a committee reviews each proposal and awards points to each section based on the criteria published in the RFP. The vendor whose proposal receives the highest score wins.
- A committee reviews each proposal and awards points to each section based on the criteria published in the RFP. The vendor whose proposal receives the highest score wins.

For commercial organizations, the process is often centered around a single decision maker:

- A single decision maker reviews each proposal and, unilaterally, decides which product or service to acquire.

- A committee reviews each proposal and makes a recommendation to the decision maker. The decision maker then decides which product or service to acquire.
- A team of subject matter experts reviews assigned sections and then makes recommendations to a single decision maker. For example, an IT expert may review the section of each proposal focused around IT security to ensure it meets requirements. He would then provide his assessment to the decision maker identifying which vendors are compliant, which aren't, etc.

The point is there isn't just one approach that buyers use to make purchase decisions. This is why it's so important to understand their decision making model; it gives you the insight to structure your proposal to match their process.

Documenting decision criteria

The decision model describes the buyer's process for making a decision. The decision criteria describes the specific things that must be included in your solution.

Most RFPs include a section describing the *official* criteria the buyer will be using to evaluate your response. For example, they may award 10 points if your headquarters is located within fifty miles of theirs. This is important information, but experienced proposal writers understand that, for every criterion, there is a backstory.

Documenting the decision criteria, and understanding the backstory for each, is one of your salesperson's most important tasks during the pre-RFP discovery phase. In the months and years before the RFP is published, your salespeople need to be asking each decision maker and influencer what these criteria are or will be and why they're important. The more you know, they more effective you'll be.

HOW IMPORTANT IS PRICE?

I've heard many salespeople claim "the only reason buyers issue RFPs is because they want the lowest price." In fact, any salesperson who employs this obsolete generality to justify dismissing the function and role of RFPs is himself irresponsible and shortsighted.

In the real world, the importance of price will vary depending on the unique goals of each procurement. In some state and local government procurements, for example, buyers are required under the law to establish which vendors meet minimum requirements, and of them, to choose the vendors with the lowest price. In this case, price is the primary issue.

There are other procurements, though, that have a different objective. I remember one recent procurement where the buyer was willing to spend far more if the vendor could produce better outcomes for their user base. It wasn't about price, it was about results.

The point is every buyer is different, every procurement is different, and if you're going to be effective at winning more of them, you must understand how important price is in their selection process.

CHAPTER RECAP

Sales are won or lost in the 12-24 months before an RFP is released. This period is also where your salespeople—or your operations staff if your company manages the current contract—collect as much information as they can about the buyer, the program, its history, and more.

No proposal writer, no matter how skilled, can write an effective or compelling proposal if she doesn't understand the nature and scope of the opportunity on which she's bidding. Do a good job collecting this information and you'll be better prepared when the time comes to write a compelling proposal.

14. Pre-Kickoff Meeting: Scrutinizing the RFP

Everybody reads an RFP, but not everybody analyzes an RFP. I am recommending you analyze each RFP with a critical eye and a systematic, almost forensic approach to learn as much as you can about what it includes.

Consider this example. Most RFPs include a short explanation of the buyer's goals or objectives for the procurement. I'm generalizing here, but in my experience, most sellers will do little more than a cursory review of said goals or objectives: *"Yea, yea, they're buying payroll services. What else?"* Then they move on, typically without giving this section any more consideration.

In contrast to this rapid review approach, you should be diving deeper. You should be reading each and every word in the goals and objectives section, and while you're doing it, you should keep asking yourself these questions:

- *What do they mean here?*
- *Why did they use that word there?*
- *They keep referring to 'accountability,' it must be important if they repeat it so often. Why is that?*

Hopefully you see where I'm going with this. Be critical. Be questioning. Be suspicious. Don't just read every word, vex over every word.

Each of the following questions serves to help you get to the essence of what they want as you scrutinize the RFP.

IS THE RFP WHAT YOU EXPECTED?

If you've been working with the buyer in the 12 to 24 months before the RFP is issued, you probably have a good understanding about what will be in the RFP based on what they told you they want. Now that the RFP is released and you scour its contents, ask yourself these two questions:

- Is there some requirement or specification you expected that was not included in the RFP?
- Is there some requirement or specification you did not expect that was included in the RFP?

Whenever you encounter RFP language you did not expect, it's usually worth your while to at least try and figure out what happened. Were you misinformed or did you misunderstand? Did something fundamental change at the last minute?

Just as important as knowing what happened is figuring out how it impacts what you're going to propose. Did the new language fundamentally alter the solution you envisioned?

Always pay special attention to last minute changes because they can suggest internal events or decisions that aren't always apparent but that can impact or alter the buyer's direction.

ARE THERE ANY "SHOWSTOPPERS"?

This question is clear and straightforward: are there any showstoppers, any major requirements that you do not or cannot provide?

They're called "showstoppers" for a reason. When you're pursuing a sales opportunity but you encounter a showstopper, everything else should stop until you figure out if you can address the requirement, and if you can, whether you want to. If you cannot or do not want to, then walk away.

I'm making such a big point about it here because I often run into opportunities in which enthusiastic salespeople push forward on opportunities, despite the presence of serious showstoppers. They do this because it's an RFP, an RFP represents an opportunity, and nobody in their right mind would ever walk away from an opportunity, right? Wrong. The reality is not every opportunity is a good opportunity, and sometimes, the most profitable customer is the one you walk away from.

LIST THE MAJOR REQUIREMENTS AND SPECIFICATIONS

Most RFPs have a section where they list all of the major requirements that every proposal must provide. *Use this list to make your list.*

In addition, as you scour through the RFP, take time to identify sections of their proposal where they say things like "the provider will," "the provider shall," "the winning bidder must…," etc. These may not be listed discreetly in the requirements section, but they are requirements, nevertheless. Make sure you identify and document them now so you'll be able to reference them in your proposal later.

HOW DO THEY EVALUATE / SCORE PROPOSALS?

Now, skip ahead to their decision criteria, to the section where they talk about how they are going to evaluate your proposal.

If your salespeople were successful during the pre-RFP selling phase of this effort, they've already identified how the buyer is going to "score" your proposal response. Read through the RFP version and reconcile the two.

If they align, great. If they don't, dig in further to understand why they don't align. Did you miss something before or did they change their evaluation approach? It's important to understand why.

IS THERE ANY LANGUAGE FAVORING A COMPETITOR?

As you scour through the RFP, do you see any questions or requirements that seem to either favor a particular vendor or disqualify a group of vendors?

- **Favor a particular vendor**. You have to know your competition well if you're going to be effective at picking these out. You have to be able to look at a question and say, "this was taken from ABC Company's sales brochure." The good news is when buyers use this approach, they're often rather clumsy. They tend to recite the other vendor's talking points or sales message just a little bit too accurately. This makes them easy to pick out.

- **Disqualifying a group of vendors.** Sometimes, buyers that favor a particular vendor don't write their RFPs to favor one vendor as much as to disqualify the other vendors who are not their favorite. If they mandate a red office copier, and only one company sells a red copier while the rest of the industry only sells blue office copiers, they effectively disqualified everyone except for the vendor they want.

When you encounter this kind of language, you can save yourself a lot of time and effort by recognizing the procurement has been preordained for someone else to win. No matter what you propose or how great your price, you've already lost and your competitor has already won.

WHAT HAS CHANGED FROM THEIR LAST RFP TO THIS ONE?

Do you save and catalogue all of the RFPs you receive? If you answer yes, kudos to you. You deserve a gold medal, an attaboy, and yes, maybe even a pay raise. If you answer no, you should start. This is _**huge**_ (and please notice _**huge**_ is bold, italic, _and_ underlined because yes, it's that huge).

When you get an RFP today, one of the top issues on your mind, or that should be on your mind, is knowing what's most important to the buyer today. There are many ways to learn this—a relationship with the decision maker being the best—but another great way is to compare and contrast today's RFP with the last one the buyer published for the same contract.

> Figure out what's different between their last RFP and the current RFP and you've found something that's important today that wasn't the last time.

Suppose the previous RFP talks about customer service response times once in the entire document. This RFP, in contrast, addresses customer service response times in five places over ten pages. Not only that, they get detailed; they ask probing questions, ask for process definitions, and require service level agreements built around response times. When you see something like this, something important has changed from the last RFP to this one. It's important because, in all likelihood, it's a pain point.

- Is the current vendor falling short or have they totally failed?
- Is there a new program manager in place that wants to emphasize vendor responsiveness?

Whatever it is, something has clearly changed and your job is to figure out what that something is. Even if you don't, though, you've still learned something valuable as you prepare to respond to this RFP; since it wasn't important before, but it is obviously important now, you had better find a way to address it prominently in your proposal.

Save past RFPs and refer to them. You'll be glad you did.

ARE THERE ANY ITEMS THAT ARE NOT CLEAR?

As you're scouring the RFP, be sure to write down any items that are not clear or that could be interpreted multiple ways. Then submit those questions to the buyer—something most RFPs allow.

One of the worst things that can happen is when you get to the writing portion of your project—after vendor questions have been submitted and responded to—and you realize you still have substantive questions.

CHAPTER RECAP

Everybody reads an RFP, but not everybody analyzes an RFP. It's important at this point, as you prepare for your kickoff meeting, to analyze the RFP in great depth. Scour it. Dissect it.

If you take the time at this stage, you can often identify important things that can help you to improve your chances.

15. Kickoff Meeting Part 1: Compiling, Organizing, and Analyzing What You Know

Proposal kickoff meetings are too administrative. Too many are focused too much on project management functions like assigning tasks and establishing deadlines than figuring out how you're going to make the sale.

Don't misunderstand the message; project management is important. Every proposal development project should have a senior manager who has the ability to hand out assignments and establish deadlines, and the authority to bring down Thor's Hammer on anyone who neglects their assigned responsibilities. It's a critical part of the overall project.

Still, an RFP is not a writing project to complete, it's a sales opportunity to win. This necessarily means kickoff meetings should have a sales strategy component in addition to an administrative component.

Sales strategy is what this chapter is about.

Compiling, organizing, and analyzing what we know

So far, your sales team has done a lot of work meeting with decision makers to document everything they could about the opportunity. Also, your proposal manager has spent considerable time analyzing the RFP to identify anything and everything he could learn from it.

Now your task is to get your entire proposal response team involved and decide how to move forward. This portion of your meeting has three fundamental tasks:

1. Brief the entire team on what you've learned.
2. Figure out what it all means.
3. Decide to bid or no bid.

1. BRIEF THE ENTIRE TEAM ON WHAT YOU'VE LEARNED

Suppose you are a young lawyer who was just hired into a big firm. But instead of being brought into a new case at the beginning, you are brought into an existing case at the end. The legal team assigned to the case has been arguing in open court for the last 30 days. They've been establishing relevant facts with the jury, building their arguments supporting why your client is innocent, and doing their best to undermine the prosecution's argument.

But here's the problem. Even though you weren't present for all of those arguments, even though you weren't witness to how they presented the facts or even what facts were presented, they're handing off the case to you to deliver the closing argument. Wait, what?

This doesn't make sense, of course, but that's exactly what we do when the salesperson hands off an RFP to the proposal team without briefing them on everything that's happened up to that point.

The proposal is the closing argument

When your staff sits down to draft a proposal in response to an RFP, their job is to present the proverbial closing argument. Recognizing this, the people who make up your proposal development team MUST be educated about everything your salespeople collected during both the pre-RFP discovery phase and your deep-dive RFP analysis. The best way to educate them, to share all of the information you collected, is to prepare a comprehensive briefing for the team.

Structuring your briefing

The briefing you prepare for your proposal development team should loosely follow both the information you collected during the pre-RFP discovery phase and the insights you gained while doing a deep dive analysis of the RFP. Use this outline as a place to start.

1. Describe the program.
   1.1. Describe the project or program.
   1.2. Explain what the buyer wants in the new program, and describe how the contract has changed over time.
   1.3. Describe any grievances you encountered or uncovered, successes they've experienced and challenges they face, and any opportunities to leverage.
2. Discuss the current vendor.
   2.1. Provide a detailed accounting of the current vendor including how well they're doing in the eyes of the decision makers.
   2.2. Identify instances where they're falling short.
   2.3. Identify instances where they're unusually strong.
   2.4. Identify opportunities where they are weak and you are strong.
   2.5. Include an accounting of the vendors who have handled the program over the years.
3. Identify the individual decision makers and the non-decision-making influencers, including the following...
   3.1. Their titles and roles.
   3.2. Their influence within the decision making process.
   3.3. Their personal vendor preferences.
   3.4. Their personal motivations and objectives.
   3.5. Their personal perceptions of risk.
   3.6. Whether they are champions, antagonists, or non-committal.
   3.7. Describe any other information you discover for each decision maker or influencer that you might be able to use, highlight, or make subtle references to in your proposal.
4. Explain the circumstances.
   4.1. Explain why they are issuing the RFP now.
   4.2. Document any relevant circumstances (a change in management, the current vendor is failing, etc.).

5. Share their decision criteria and selection process.
    5.1. Identify the model or process they are using to choose a vendor or product.
    5.2. Document the criteria they will be using to make a purchase decision.
    5.3. Explain their point scoring system/award process and your evaluation of it.
6. Share observations from the RFP assessment.
    6.1. Describe any RFP content you did not expect.
    6.2. Identify any "showstoppers" you discovered.
    6.3. List the major requirements and specs they list in their RFP, and whether there was anything that diverged from your expectations.
    6.4. Identify any language that favors or appears to favor a competitor.
    6.5. Present any RFP language that changed from their last RFP to this one.
    6.6. Identify any RFP language or requirements that are not clear and need to be clarified.
7. Share anything else that is relevant.

This outline is a good place to begin, but it isn't written in stone. However you choose to organize it, it's critical the briefing you prepare is sufficiently comprehensive that your proposal development staff is fully informed. Only then will they be able to craft persuasive, customer-focused content that influences decision makers.

2. FIGURE OUT WHAT IT ALL MEANS

Now that you've collected and briefed the entire team on the opportunity, your next challenge is to lead the team in analyzing all of the information you've collected. This means you need to discuss it, vex over it, argue about it, and ultimately, process it into actionable intelligence.

The process for doing this is to ask a bunch of questions that your team, as a group, has to answer. It's important to recognize, though, that the goal is not only getting an answer; the consideration that goes into getting an answer is just as important. Your goal is to encourage the entire proposal team to discuss the opportunity and, as a group, to agree on what the customer's issues and problems and general circumstances are.

What is the buyer's primary issue/ problem/ objective?

For every procurement, there are almost always a number of things that are important to the buyer, but in my experience, there's almost always one primary issue that is driving it. Step one in your analysis is to identify that one primary issue. This is so important because this issue, and how you solve it, is going to be the central theme of your proposal.

As you work through this discussion, though, make sure you articulate the primary issue with specificity. Generalities don't work. Consider this example.

Generic: This buyer wants to buy a car that is safe.

Specific: The buyer is a dad, and his daughter is a new driver. He wants her to have a safe car while she's learning how to drive.

Even better: The buyer is a dad, and his daughter is a new driver. When dad's son was learning how to drive a few years before, he was in a terrible wreck and spent weeks recovering. Dad doesn't want to go through that again. Therefore, Dad wants his daughter to have a car that is supremely safe while she's mastering driving.

As a professional salesperson and proposal writer, I cannot sell very effectively to the generic statement. When all we have to work with are generalities, all we can respond with are more generalities. In contrast, I can sell effectively to the second statement, and I can do even better selling to the third. As a salesperson, it gives me the insight I need to build my sales message around what's important to him, that's specific to him, not some generic and disconnected message.

When your staff sits down to write proposal content, they're in the same position. They can't write well to generic descriptions, they need specifics. When you provide them specifics, they'll have what they need to write to the unique needs of the buyer.

Here's another example that is more proposal-related.

Generic: The buyer wants to replace their existing payroll processing vendor.

Specific: Their company has been expanding both in size and geography. The payroll processing vendor they've been using is a small, local business, and not equipped to handle their expansion. They are looking for a new payroll processing vendor that is large enough to handle their needs as they grow, but still offer local support in each of the cities where they operate.

To restate, your staff cannot sell effectively if the only intelligence they have to work with is the generic statement. But there's a lot an accomplished writer can do with the second, more specific statement. Your writers can talk about right-sizing your service today, and adjusting it as the buyer continues to grow. Your writers can draw a map of the buyer's offices next to your offices, and even introduce the senior people in each of your offices that will provide direct support to each of their offices. Your writers could talk about how even though you are a much larger payroll processing company than the firm they're currently using, they will continue to get the same kind of focused, one-to-one, hand-holding support they're accustomed to.

Whether you're a sales professional selling in person or a proposal writer drafting content, the more you know about the buyer and their story, the more specific the information you get, the more effectively you will be able to craft a targeted and customer-focused sales message.

What are their next five major issues and requirements?

So far, we discussed how procurements are usually driven by one primary issue, problem, or objective. Once a decision is made to procure a product or service, though, there are often other important issues or requirements that factor into the decision-making process.

As a proposal strategy team, you need to discuss and agree what the top five issues and requirements are. Sure, there may be more than five, but try to limit this list to the top five most important things that influence the buyer's decision making.

In the car buying example above, the primary consideration is dad finding a car that's super safe for his daughter who's learning how to drive. This predicates everything else. Once this primary requirement has been fulfilled, though, dad piles on a few other things:

- The car should be red.
- The price should be under $10K.
- No tinted windows.
- No fancy stereo system.
- Must have ABS brakes.

The primary issue is a requirement; dad won't buy the car if it's not safe. These five additional "requirements" are more negotiable. If it has everything else except it's blue instead of red, he may still buy the car. If it's $11K instead of $10K, he may still buy the car.

In the previous payroll processing example, the buyer's primary issue is to find a payroll processing company that can service their organization as they expand in both size and geographic footprint. Once this primary requirement is fulfilled, there are some other things they also want their vendor to provide:

- The ability to distribute payroll as paper checks, pay cards, or direct deposit.
- The ability to accept and process an array of payroll file types, from timekeeping systems to Excel spreadsheets to flat files.
- Easy access to veteran professionals who have both the knowledge and authority to fix problems quickly.
- Patient, helpful service—hand holding—so their less-experienced staff can setup new employees with minimal effort or frustration.
- A willingness to provide their staff with quarterly briefings on changes to regulations or tax laws that impact their business or employees.

These things are important to the buyer, and any vendor they select will necessarily have to offer all or most of these requirements. Therefore, everyone who is in your kickoff meeting, and involved at some level in the proposal development process, must understand the importance of these requirements. This is because later, when your staff is drafting content, they need to incorporate these ideas throughout the response.

This is important.

You don't just talk about customer service when answering a question about customer service. If customer service is a requirement for the buyer, if it's important to them, you should find ways to reference customer service in strategic places throughout your response. For example, the payroll customer we've been discussing may ask whether you have an office in Dayton. Most proposal writers would respond by saying, "Yes, we have an office in Dayton." But you're different. From all of the sales work you've done, you know that Dayton is one of their remote offices where they don't have a lot of technical staff. Therefore, instead of just saying, "Yes, we have an office in Dayton," you might consider drafting content that addresses this issue:

> *Yes, we have an office in Dayton. Moreover, the office is run by Jane Smith. Jane is recognized internally, and among our client base in Dayton, for her ability to make it as easy and simple as possible for new clients to transition to our service.*

It's a few more words, sure, but it also succinctly and effectively addresses one of their top issues. And if the head of their Dayton office reads it, it's a homerun.

How important is price in their decision?

During the pre-RFP discovery phase, your salesperson worked to understand the role of price in the buyer's decision. Now it's time to share that understanding with the proposal development team.

If price is their most important criteria, then configure your solution so you can offer a lower price. If you either cannot do that or don't want to, then walk away.

If something else is more important than price, the team needs to know about that. Price is always an issue at some level, so don't disregard it completely, but make certain your solution emphasizes whatever it is they want most so you'll be able to justify the price you charge.

Whatever you decide, make certain everyone on the team understands the relative importance of price in the buyer's decision making process.

What is your strategy in response to their selection process?

During the pre-RFP discovery effort, your salesperson identified the process the buyer is using to make their purchase decision. In the first part of this meeting you shared this information with the team.

Now the exercise before the team is to decide what strategy you're going to use as you craft your response.

This is important. If your selling approach doesn't match their buying process, you aren't speaking the same language, you've missed the boat, you're barking up the wrong tree.

Consider these examples.

The vendor with the most points wins

The buyer is a state or local government agency. They established the selection process so a committee reviews each proposal and awards points for each section based on how well the proposal addresses their needs. The vendor whose proposal receives the highest score wins.

In this scenario, value is incorporated into their buying process. They don't just ask, "does this meet our minimum qualifications?" They are exploring which proposal offers them the best overall outcome, the best value.

Your selling strategy, therefore, is to make your proposal customer-focused, promote the value you provide, explain how your solution is both different and better than the competitions', etc.

Minimum qualifications, lowest price

The buyer is a state or local government agency. The selection process they use is for a procurement person to first evaluate each proposal to determine whether it satisfies minimum RFP requirements. If it does, a second person will then rank the proposals according to which has the lowest price.

It's important to recognize that if the buyer is using this buying model, value does not matter like it does in the previous example. Not even a little bit. In this scenario, they don't care if you have the best staff, the most experience, deliver better outcomes, or that you invested $1M to redesign your infrastructure so you provide better quality. None of that matters. ALL they care about is whether you meet the minimum qualifications (yes or no), and if you do, whether your price is the lowest. That's it.

Your strategy, therefore, is to make certain you satisfy all of their minimum stated requirements, and then sharpen your pencil so you can present the lowest possible price. Nothing else matters.

A single decision maker makes the purchase decision

Most commonly encountered in a commercial environment, a single decision maker is tasked with making the decision. Sometimes, this person makes the decision without any input. More commonly, this person might decide after receiving input from other people or groups within the organization. Either way, decision authority rests with this one person.

Your strategy, therefore, is to make certain your proposal addresses all of the things that, through discovery, you have learned are most important to this individual.

Adjusting your strategy

The point of this entire discussion is that your strategy for approaching each RFP is to match the selection/decision model the buyer is using. If it doesn't, you're wasting time and resources.

How do you maximize the points you can earn?

In the last chapter, when you scrutinized the RFP, you documented how the buyer is assigning points. In the kickoff meeting, your job now is to customize your proposal strategy so you will win every possible point you can. To do this, I've found it effective to ask a series of questions to the entire proposal development team in an effort to make sure everyone is in agreement with what is most important.

Where is the buyer awarding the most points? The least?

This is straightforward. Are they awarding the most points for price? For quality of the solution? For flexibility of your service team?

Likewise, ask where they're awarding the least number of points. If they are awarding almost no points for price, but a lot of points for the quality of the solution or a bidder's credentials, then don't spend much time talking about how your solution is cost effective.

By working through this exercise, you will be getting your entire team focused on what things are the most important to stress in your proposal content so you earn the most points when the buyer scores it.

Get creative about earning points

I once worked on an RFP response where a big chunk of the points was being awarded if you could show you were a local vendor. The service provider I was working with was based in another state and did not have a local office. I naturally assumed we would not be getting those points. My customer, though, was smarter and more creative than me.

He researched what was legally required to claim you were local, and therefore, earn the points. He discovered all you had to do was to have a local utilities account. Learning this, and realizing those points could tip the balance of the procurement, he rented a shed and signed up for utilities there so he could claim he was local and get the points.

It was a brilliant idea. With a couple hundred dollar investment, he was able to earn points that none of the other non-local service providers could claim.

This is just one example, but it demonstrates how a little inventiveness can win you points you might otherwise forego.

3. DECIDE TO BID OR NO-BID

One of the best ways to improve your proposal win rate is to not bid on every RFP that comes in the door. Large federal contractors with large, mature business and proposal development programs already know this.

An associate of mine calls this, "chasing rabbits." These federal contractors know if they don't waste time chasing opportunities they're unlikely to win, chasing rabbits, they are not only going to reduce their losses and improve their win rate, they're also going to save a lot of time and effort they can invest in opportunities they have a legitimate shot at winning.

In my experience dealing with small and mid-size businesses, though, the attitude is often very different. They often respond to almost every RFP, even in cases where their chances of winning are slim to non-existent. One business explained their approach by restating what the company president once said to them, "You can't win if you don't bid." They now use this philosophy to justify responding to almost *everything*—even opportunities where they are clearly unqualified.

Some businesses bid because they don't know any better

Why bid on an opportunity you aren't going to win? For some, it's because managers do not understand the reality of the formal procurement process. Specifically, they do not understand that if they do not have a relationship with a buyer before the RFP is issued, their chance of winning is low—*single digits low*. They bid because they are bamboozled into believing an RFP received "out of the blue" is a legitimate opportunity. They're wrong, they lose, and they waste a lot of resources doing it.

Some businesses bid because managers are scared not to

Most proposal managers understand the futility of responding to an RFP they are unlikely to win. Interestingly, though, most know the ones they are likely going to lose, but they respond anyway. In my experience, there are often two reasons why this happens.

First, the sales team pushes to pursue every RFP that comes in the door because it doesn't cost them anything, personally. "The RFP represents an opportunity," they reason, "so why wouldn't we respond?" Even though they have no relationship with the buyer, even though they know hardly anything about the opportunity or the decision makers or why it's going out to bid now, they push for the proposal team to pursue the opportunity. And why wouldn't they? After all, they still get a commission if it closes, even though they haven't done any work. Regardless, this shortsighted approach is a great, big, huge, grand waste of resources.

Second, managers respond to RFPs even when they know they're going to lose because they're scared not to. They worry they'll be criticized for not pursuing opportunities, and in organizations where senior managers take the shortsighted philosophy "you can't win if you don't bid," they may be correct. So they invest a lot of resources crafting a proposal they know they're going to lose. And then they lose.

Build a bid/no bid decision gate into your process

Large federal contractors have sophisticated systems they use to decide whether to respond to an RFP opportunity. Small and midsize sellers can't generally afford these sophisticated and sometimes very complex systems.

For most small and midsize businesses, though, you don't need such complexity. It's often enough to ask the question, "is this RFP worth pursuing or is it a waste of time?"

Once you take this first, simple step, then you can add a few questions to bolster your decision process:

- Did we know about this RFP before we received it?
- Do we know anything about this opportunity other than what we learned from the RFP?
- Do we have any kind of substantive relationship with any of the central decision makers in this buyer's organization?
- Is there any strategic reason we should be responding to this RFP even if we know we're likely going to lose?

If you answer no to anyone of these questions, you should seriously consider not responding. Seriously consider. Not responding. Really.

As you spend more time refining your bid/no bid decision process, there are many more criteria and considerations you may want to incorporate, but that comes later. The first thing right now is making sure you at least have a decision gate, a stop point, where someone knows to ask, where someone is allowed to ask, "Should we even be responding to this RFP?"

Where in the process does the bid/no bid decision happen?

Good question!

I include the bid/no bid decision in this chapter, towards the end of the kickoff meeting, because I wasn't really sure where else to put it. In fact, though it should be included as a decision gate at one or more points in your larger business development process, anyone involved in your business development effort should have the right to raise his or her hand, stop progress, and ask the question that everyone involved in the effort is then obliged to address: "Wait, the more I learn about this opportunity, it doesn't seem like it's a good fit for us. Can we have a meeting to discuss whether to pursue it?"

The best way to improve your win rate is to stop chasing rabbits you aren't going to catch, and stop chasing opportunities you have no chance of winning. Embrace this one simple idea and you are going to not only improve your win rate, you are going to save money, reduce frustration among your staff, and free up more resources to invest in the opportunities you have a legitimate chance at winning.

CHAPTER RECAP

At some point in every business development project, you have to pull all of the information together into a single place. You have to document it, discuss it, analyze it, consider it, argue about it, evaluate it, reevaluate it, and if you're good and a little bit lucky, figure out what it all means.

Just as important, everyone on your team who is going to be involved in writing part of your proposal must understand the totality of this discussion. They have to be a part of it as it develops. They need to understand. Only then will they be ready and able to write compelling content in response to it. Only then will they be able to write your closing argument.

16. Kickoff Meeting Part 2: Configuring Your Solution

Back in the day, we used to sell products and services. Then some bright person came along and introduced a new idea into the professional discourse; we weren't selling products or services, we learned, we were selling solutions to buyers' problems.

This was a revolutionary idea back then, and it demonstrated clearly how the sales profession was growing and evolving. After this latest revelation, we were no longer just pushing products down the channel, we were acting like consultants. We were becoming professional problem solvers, and our stated purpose was to address the unique problems and challenges our customers faced.

Unfortunately, it wasn't too long after the solution concept was introduced that everyone started substituting the word solution whenever they were talking about their product or service. Sellers were wrong to do this then, and they still are today; products and solutions are not synonyms, and we should not treat them as if they are.

A product is a product. A service is a service. A solution is something we build for a client who is trying to solve a problem. The solution may include one or more of our products or services, along with other things, but they are each unique things.

SELLING SOLUTIONS VS. PRODUCTS—AN EXAMPLE

You sell office copiers. You've got big copiers, small copiers, red copiers, blue copiers, standalone copiers, networked copiers—all kinds of copiers. These copiers are not your solution, per se, they are the machines that make up your product line. OK so far?

You may sell the exact same copier to three unique businesses, but you are not selling the same solution to each buyer. In the three fictional examples below, each customer is unique, and each requires a unique solution custom built for their needs.

- Sally at Mom's Corner Store needs a small, inexpensive copier that she can use to receive faxes from her vendors and make copies of invoices before she mails them out to her credit customers. She needs an installment payment plan because she doesn't have lots of cash flow. She also needs someone who can setup the machine because, while she's great at running a general store, she doesn't know a thing about electronics.

- Jack at the local library needs the same copier as Sally, but he needs a coin device attached to it so people can pay to make copies. He's pretty good with the maintenance part of it, he can set it up himself and replenish the paper and toner, but because it's a revenue source for the library, he needs prompt service if the copier ever breaks.

- Suzy runs a small mortgage closing agency and is required, by law, to provide each client with a copy of each document at the closing, before they leave her office. She doesn't have a huge volume of business—she is semi-retired, after all—but whatever she buys, she needs the confidence that her copier will always be working when she needs it so she'll never have to reschedule a closing.

These are simple examples, but they illustrate the point well. You are selling the exact same copier to each buyer, but if you're doing your job well, you are packaging that copier in a solution wrapper that is built custom for each buyer.

- For Sally, you include a 12 months same as cash program so she can afford it, you agree to deliver it and set it up for her, and you agree to stop by and replace her toner cartridge when it gets low.

- For Jack, you attach a coin-operated device so people at the library can pay to make copies. You also include your one-hour response service plan so if the copier ever stops working, someone is there to fix it within the hour. One final thing—and the one thing Jack appreciates more than the rest—you offer to pass out flyers around town to help get out the word about the library's new pay-to-make-copies service.

- For Suzy, you're providing the same copier you did for Sally and Jack, but you propose two copiers instead of just one. This redundancy means she will never have to reschedule a mortgage closing because her copier isn't working.

See the point? You're selling the same copier to each customer, but because they each have different requirements, you've created a solution unique to each.

WHY IS ALL THIS IMPORTANT IN AN RFP/PROPOSAL CONTEXT?

When an organization gets an RFP, too many sellers are too quick to sit down and start typing answers to questions. They don't take the time to figure out what they're selling—the actual solution they're going to propose—before they dive into messaging. In other words, they're just selling a product or service, not a custom solution tailored to a specific client.

I was explaining this concept to one client and he pushed back: "We sell data support services. It doesn't matter who we're selling to, we sell the same basic service." Whenever someone says something like this, my initial reaction is he hasn't dug deep enough to find out more about the customer, their needs and concerns, and how he can appeal to what's important to them. So that's what we did, we dug deeper.

Before long, our effort produced results. We learned the manager who leads their support group was well known to the buyer; he had actually worked for the buyer in an earlier job. Further, the buyer thinks highly of him and his abilities. Once we learned this tidbit, we made this manager an integral part of the solution we were proposing. He was skilled and able, talented at solving problems remotely, and because he had worked there, he was already familiar with the buyer's firm. This manager's involvement ultimately turned out to be a large and compelling component of the solution we were proposing.

The point is you can't just sell the same product or service to every client and call it a solution. You actually have to take time to configure a unique solution for each unique client—and you need to do this before you start working on messaging. This is precisely what this portion of your kickoff meeting is focused on doing.

1. Configure and summarize the solution

This is where your business development team creates and drafts the solution you want to propose. Your solution should mention all of the relevant components the customer will want to know about.

Please note we are not yet discussing messaging, that comes later. All we're doing now is documenting the solution that will address what the buyer said she wants. Here's how we might structure a solution for Suzy at Suzy's Mortgage Closing Service.

- *The solution we are proposing to Suzy's Mortgage Closing Service includes two OfficeMaster5000 copiers. Having two identical copiers ensures she never has to postpone a mortgage closing because a copier isn't working.*
- *Sam will be doing the installation. Sam has done copier service work for Suzy before and she respects his ability. They like each other and get along well.*
- *Though we are proposing two copiers, we were able to save her money by charging for the basic service plan, not the premium plan. Since our solution includes a backup copier, it's not imperative for her to have one-hour service if one of the copiers breaks. This, alone, makes our solution closer in price to the single copier plus one-hour service option she had previously been considering.*
- *We're giving her a 7% manufacturer's discount because she's buying two machines. This, and the savings from the basic service plan, puts our solution in the same ball park with the competition—despite the redundancy of having two copiers—which she likes.*
- *We're promising delivery within a week of signing the contract. Our competitor is quoting her a three-week delivery on their machine.*

This is obviously a fictional and simple example, but it illustrates the point. It's important not just to document the solution, it's important that everyone in your kickoff meeting understands the solution we're proposing and the story behind it. With this knowledge and background, when they sit down to write their assigned sections, they're able to draft content that is more customer-focused.

2. Include non-traditional components that add value

When we think like sellers, we often think in terms of what we're selling. When we think like buyer's, though, we tend to view what we're buying in a more comprehensive, holistic way—not just what we're buying but the totality of what we get.

> It's not about what we're selling, it's about the totality of what they get.

Sometimes, often times, the things buyers value most have nothing to do with the product or service we're selling but the little things that make their lives easier. Here are a few examples.

Notification of legislative or regulatory updates

One of my clients operated in an industry that was heavily regulated by the federal government and separately by each state government. Because they were a national organization, they tracked and compiled all of the regulations and court decisions both at the federal and the state level. What's great is they shared what they collected with their clients.

Their clients did not pay for this information, they paid for a separate, related service. But this information still proved valuable to the buyers who received it. They were able to use it and benefit from it, even though they didn't actually pay for it.

It's not what you're selling, it's what they get.

An invoicing department that's easy to work with

One client I worked with had a client base made up entirely of small organizations with relatively limited internal resources. After interviewing some of these small-organization clients, we learned that one of the things they liked most about us was how easy we were to work with. And this sentiment was most pronounced in our invoicing practices.

In this particular industry, there are many line items that make up an invoice. My client had a sophisticated system to track each line item, and then to present them to their client in a way that was easy to understand. They also had a great service in place where their clients could call Janice to ask about individual items. Janice was great and easy going, likeable, and more important, she was a wiz at quickly figuring out whatever question or issue the buyer raised. This made it easy on the buyer's limited-resource accounting department—something the buyers very much appreciated. It was incidental to my client's offering, but it was huge to their customers.

It's not what you're selling, it's what they get.

CHAPTER RECAP

Most sellers don't take the time to build a solution for a buyer, they just start writing about the product or service they're selling. This is a mistake.

You aren't selling a product or a service, you're selling a solution, and you must take the time to figure out what that solution is before you start writing about it. Figure it out, make sure all of your proposal development staff shares your vision, and only then can you begin drafting persuasive proposal content.

17. Kickoff Meeting Part 3: Configuring Your Sales Message

So far, we've spent considerable time in our kickoff meeting understanding the circumstances surrounding the bid, discussing the buyer and their needs, and configuring the solution we want to propose. As we transition into this next phase of the meeting, our goal is to decide how we want to communicate our solution to the buyer.

To be clear, the solution we create is different from the messaging we use to communicate it. The *solution* solves their problem, but the *messaging* is how we explain it to them; it's the way we tell them how our solution is going to get them what they want.

PROCESS AND OUTCOME

The process we use during this phase of our meeting is to ask a series of questions. The outcome we hope to achieve from this process is to create a list of talking points that all of our staff can refer to when drafting content.

Process: asking questions

In modern Western culture, we routinely use the term *dialogue* interchangeably with words like conversation, a discussion between two or more people. In our kickoff meeting, though, I want to use it more like Socrates and Plato did, as a didactic or learning device built around conversational exchange. In other words, *thinking out loud together*.

The way this works, I offer a comment or observation about something. You hear what I'm saying and respond, "Yea, I see where you're going with this. What if we did this..." Then someone else chimes in, "Yes, we're redefining the problem. I like this. How about we say it this way..." And then we're off, working cooperatively, as a team, throwing out ideas, considering different perspectives, etc. See the point? We're working together as a team to use our collective creativity to build a better solution; *we're thinking out loud together.*

This chapter includes a list of questions intended to inspire this dialogue. As you review these questions, please remember that our primary goal is not a quick answer; that completely undermines the purpose of this phase of the meeting. Messaging is not about efficiency, it's about effectiveness. Dig in deep. Entertain new ideas. Explore new perspectives. The more you discuss it, the better your message will become.

Outcome: talking points

One of the best ways to configure your sales message for this kind of project is to create a series of talking points. This is just like the talking points you always hear about on political news shows. We are boiling down your story, your message, into a list of concise sentences or phrases that are easy to recall and then articulate.

Then, everyone who leaves the meeting will have a list of the exact same talking points so we're all communicating the exact same message.

Using an example opportunity to explain

In my experience teaching this section in training classes—trying to illustrate both the process and the talking points we produce—I've found it much easier if we have an example opportunity to pursue. So before we slog ahead, let's pause a moment and draft an example opportunity we can use to explore this approach.

Example opportunity: Donna's Fictional Coffee Cups wants a payroll solution

We are Dave's Fictional Payroll Processing Company and we are trying to make a sale to Donna's Fictional Coffee Cups. Earlier in our kickoff meeting, we identified Donna's primary reason for issuing the RFP; they're expanding and they need a payroll company that can keep up.

Donna's has been expanding both in size and geography. The payroll processing vendor they've been using is a small, local shop, and not well equipped to handle their expansion. They're looking for a new payroll processing vendor that is large enough to handle their needs as they grow but is still able to provide local support in each of the cities where they operate.

Because we understand Donna's objectives so well, we configured a solution to ensure they get what they want. We defined it this way.

We are assigning Bob, one of our senior veteran operations staff, to be the primary account manager to Donna's central office. Bob already has a working relationship with the controller there, Sally. They know each other through a number of shared associations, and they previously worked at the same accounting department in the same company.

The RFP says they have seven offices in as many cities. In the solution we configured, we are proposing that each of our office managers in each of those cities are assigned to each senior manager in each of their offices. Further, each of these office managers becomes a part of the account team under Bob's leadership. Their senior managers were not listed in the RFP, but we identified them previously and reached out to each of them over the last six months to introduce ourselves, so they know who we are.

City	Our account staff	Their senior manager at that office
Cincinnati	Bob Jones	Sally Smith
Columbus	Joe Johnson	Barb Bartinelli
Cleveland	Lisa Lo	Chris Crane
Indianapolis	Paul Puff	Doug Double
Lexington	Carol Comber	Suzy Sierra
Louisville	Jamie Jesse	Tracey Tongo
Chicago	Becky Beaufort	Chris Calico

This arrangement will satisfy their primary requirement; a. that we're large enough to serve all of their offices as they expand, and b. that we have a local account team in place to provide personalized service to each office.

Now that we've defined our example opportunity, including the problem they're experiencing and the solution we've configured to address it, we can advance to the subject of this chapter—*messaging*. Specifically, we need to figure out how to create and communicate a sales message they will find compelling.

QUESTIONS TO ASK

As in other parts of the kickoff meeting, our process here is to ask a series of questions. Remember our purpose for asking questions is not to get quick answers but to inspire dialogue. We want to encourage each member of our business development team, including each person helping to develop content, to participate and contribute to the discussion.

1. How is the solution we are proposing going to address the buyer's primary issue?

In answering this first question, in building our talking points, we need to fill out a table with three columns:
- The customer's issue
- Our solution
- The benefit the buyer receives

It's important to summarize our comments into concise snippets. You can get really detailed, if you want, but I advise you resist the temptation. Everyone who is going to be reviewing these talking points has been participating in the meeting so you don't have to recap every detail. Fewer points, clearly stated, make it easier for your writers to draft compelling, customer-focused content.

The customer's issue	Our approach	The benefit the customer receives
They want coverage today	We mapped each of our offices to each of their offices in each city. We have the geographic coverage to serve their entire organization today.	*No delay or ramp up. We have the infrastructure, in place today, to serve your needs.*
Coverage as they expand	We identified the cities they are planning to expand into over the next 36 months. We confirmed we now have, or will have, offices in each of those cities.	*No uncertainty or unpredictability; we have or will have the infrastructure to serve your future offices as they come online.*
Local support for each office	We built an account team, headed by Bob, that provides for each local office manager to work individually with each of their office managers at each of their locations. That equals local support.	*You aren't losing anything by switching to a larger firm. Even though we are larger than your current vendor, we have the local support to provide personal service to each office across your enterprise.*

This simple table fully encapsulates the messaging we want to communicate whenever we're discussing their primary issue.

2. Focus on the other buying requirements: how are we going to address/solve the top five?

Just like we created talking points for their main issue, we must also create talking points for each of the secondary issues they care about. We need to start by acknowledging the buyer's issue, then summarizing our response, and then articulating what they get by choosing our solution.

Getting back to our payroll example

In an earlier segment of our sales proposal meeting, we identified the five secondary issues that our buyer, Donna's Fictional Coffee Cups, is seeking from any solution we build for them:

- The vendor must offer checks, pay cards, and direct deposit.
- The vendor must be able to accept and process a broad array of files types from timekeeping systems to Excel spreadsheets to flat files.
- Their staff must have easy access to managers who have both the knowledge and authority to fix problems quickly.
- Especially for some of their smaller, remote offices, the vendor must provide patient, helpful service—hand holding—so their less-experienced staff can setup new employees with minimal effort or frustration.
- The vendor must provide their staff with quarterly briefings on changes to regulations or tax laws that impact their business or employees.

Our goal here is to create talking points for each of the secondary issues that are important to the buyer.

Their issue	Our approach	The benefit the customer receives
Each employee should be able to choose how they are paid.	Each employee can choose their own method of compensation; a paper check, a debit card, or an electronic deposit directly into their account.	*Not all of your employees have checking accounts, and it costs them to go somewhere to cash their paychecks. With payment cards, they can now have access to their full pay without penalty.*

Across their organization, their offices submit payroll in three different file types.	We can accept payroll files in a wide variety of formats, from electronic transfer to manual submission.	*Until you consolidate to a single format, none of your offices has to change how they submit payroll records. We accept them all, and we have systems in place to ensure each transmission was received accurately. This minimizes the time you have to invest in reconciliation and recovery.*
Access to authority to fix problems.	Your program manager has a direct line to our senior operations manager.	*If you ever encounter a problem, and you aren't satisfied with how we solved it at your local office, you can call Jane, our VP of Operations. Jane has the authority, expertise, and motivation to fix it and make you happy.*
"Hand holding" level service for remote offices.	We have included our senior office managers, in each city where your offices are located, as part of our account team.	*Each of our managers in each of the cities where you operate will reach out to your staff to build a working, one-on-one relationship. If any of them ever have an issue, our local office manager will personally walk them through to resolution.*
Regular regulatory updates.	As a normal course of our payroll business, we monitor legislative and regulatory changes. As a client, we share our findings with you.	*You will always be aware of the most recent changes to laws or regulations that impact your operations. This helps you stay compliant without costing you anything additional.*

3. What advantages do we have, within the context of this particular opportunity, compared to the competition?

We've discussed in previous sections about differentiators, business strengths, unique competitive advantages—or whatever we're choosing to call them today. These are the things that make us both different and better than the competition.

The problem most sellers have is they tend to define differentiators at a marketing level instead of a solution level. What we want to do when answering this question, though, is to get more specific and more customer-focused.

What makes us different and better? Good question. What makes us different and better in the eyes of this buyer? Great question.

Unique competitive advantage	Explanation	The message...
They love our account manager, Bob	They've been working with Bob for many years. They know him and they trust him. They want to keep working with him.	*Bob is our employee. If they work with us, they get to work with Bob. None of our competitors have Bob.*
Geographic proximity	We have an office within 10 miles of each of their offices. We also have offices in the three cities they're thinking of expanding into.	*Unlike some other payroll processing firms that lack local presence, our close proximity means we can be more responsive to their needs; if they have an issue, we can be onsite within an hour.*

New invoicing system streamlines invoicing and payment	We have a new, state of the art accounting and invoicing system that streamlines the entire invoicing and payment process. This is one of the things they've been complaining about with their current vendor, that their vendor's system is error-prone, and if they have questions, it's difficult for them to find answers.	*Unlike their current vendor, our new system will improve accuracy and minimize their administrative overhead reconciling invoicing issues.*

When your staff walks out of this meeting and back to their cubicles, these talking points make certain they clearly understand the things that make us different and better than the competition.

4. What are our competitors' advantages compared to us? How are we going to overcome them?

As we work our way through our messaging discussion, we need to spend at least some time talking about our competitors, the advantages they have or may claim to have over us, and how we are going to undermine or minimize their claims.

Many sellers don't like this exercise. When you're focusing on their advantages over you, it feels defeatist. It's almost like you're rooting for the other team. Still, it's a powerful and effective exercise if you're willing to make the effort and learn from it. It will allow you to more intelligently position your solutions against your competitors' solutions.

You need to build a table that has three columns:

- The competitors' advantages
- An explanation
- How you are going to address it

The Competitors' Advantages	Explanation	How we address it
They offer a lower price	XYZ Payroll company offers a lower price for their basic service, but they nickel and dime for every additional service you want.	*It's important to compare apples to apples. Our price may appear higher than some of our competitors, but we charge one flat fee for our service. Unlike some others, we never charge for extra file types or payment methods. With our service, you can budget more accurately and predictably.*
They are significantly larger than we are	Their company is huge. They have lots of cash, lots of resources, lots of people, and they have name brand recognition in the larger market.	*While some of our competitors may be larger, don't get confused because that's not comparing apples to apples. Their payroll processing group, which is one small division of their overall enterprise, is about the same size as our company. In other words, they aren't any larger than we are, but unlike them, our entire business is focused on payroll services for companies like yours.*

If you are going to tell the buyer how your solution is different and better, you should expect your competitor will do the same. If you can ghost the competition, though, if you can show the weaknesses of their arguments and provide information that will prompt the buyer to ask more questions of your competition, you will advance your cause.

5. What shortcomings do we have to overcome? How are we going to overcome them?

As a proposal consultant with years of experience working for many sellers, I can tell you with certainty that I have never seen a perfect solution. Every solution has a shortcoming or a blemish or an ugly wart. Some are even plagued with afflictions so severe they're deal breakers.

As a team, you need to identify these shortcomings, you need to agree how serious they are, and then you need to figure out how you're going to address them. The table below is one way to organize this information.

Shortcoming	Seriousness	How we address it
They have expressed interest in expanding into Canada at some point in the future. They want a vendor that can support them there.	**Not too serious**. Their conversations about this have so far been casual, but no real plans and no real determination. Advise we don't even address it unless we have to.	*If it does come up…"Like you, we have also considered expanding our business into Canada. Though we aren't there now, we have done considerable research already, and we could implement an expansion with relatively little delay."*
They require we have an independent audit to confirm we have security measures in place to protect their employees' data.	**Serious**. We have security measures, and we just hired a Security Officer to bolster our security program, but have not yet engaged an outside organization to perform an audit.	*1. Admit we don't have external certification today. 2. Explain what we have done (robust security infrastructure, hiring a new security officer, etc.). 3. Promise to engage an external security audit within three months of being awarded the contract. 4. Emphasize we have never had a security breach in our ten years in business.*

If it's a relatively insignificant shortcoming, maybe you choose to not say anything. If it's a major shortcoming, though, not saying anything is like trying to host a cocktail party with a great, big elephant standing in the middle of the room. It's useless to ignore the elephant, especially when everyone sees him (and probably smells him, too). You have to figure out how to address it. If it's a really huge shortcoming, maybe you choose not to respond.

Just make sure everyone on your team understands the shortcomings and how you're going to address them before they go off to write their proposal content sections.

6. What do they perceive are their greatest risks? How are we going to defuse those perceptions?

In an earlier part of our meeting, we identified perceptions of risk within the buyer's organization. Now, in the messaging portion of the meeting, we have to figure out how we're going to address those perceptions.

Identified Risk	Source	How we address it
Concern about the size and stability of the company they hire. The last two firms they hired went out of business before the contract was complete.	A generalized concern across the organization, though the loudest voice is Sally's in accounting. She's the one who's had to fix everything after the other two firms went out of business.	*We need to stress that we are a stable organization. 1. We are profitable, and have been every year since we launched. 2. We are growing, but we regulate our growth so we don't suffer cash flow problems. 3. We have a $5M line of credit, but we have no debt. We are a stable and ongoing concern.*

7. What is our style and tone?

Have you ever read a proposal that appears as though it was written by ten different people? It probably was, but it shouldn't sound that way. It should sound like it was written by a single person using a consistent style and tone. Clearly, it's difficult to make a single document with multiple authors sound like it was written by one, but there are a few things you can do to improve your chances.

Use present tense most of the time

The popular style manuals handle this question differently. For proposal writing, though, I recommend using present tense most of the time because it sounds more decisive, more certain. Consider these examples.

- **Future tense**: The payroll program we are proposing will provide a better way to reconcile your payroll files with actual payables.
- **Present tense**: The payroll program we are proposing provides a better way to reconcile your payroll files with actual payables.

I know, I know, it's a small detail. And admittedly, you aren't going to win a deal just by switching all of your writing to present tense from future tense. Still, writing in present tense sounds stronger, and like I said, more certain. It's the difference between, "we do this already," and "if you hire us, we promise to do this."

Whatever you decide, make sure everyone uses the same tense.

Use active voice

On the Association of Proposal Management Professionals (APMP) discussion board some years back, there was a conversation about active voice vs. passive voice. One discussion participant, Frank Karlin, illustrated well what it sounds like when you're using the passive. I'm paraphrasing, but he suggested the next time you leave for work in the morning, try saying something like this:

You are loved, and will be seen tonight.

I laughed out loud when I read this, and I can almost hear the startled response: "Wait! I am loved? By whom? And who's going to see me tonight? Come back here and explain yourself!"

We've all been taught to write in active voice, and this humorous example clarifies why. Passively written sentences are squirrely and unclear. They're ambiguous. In fact, they're only useful when your goal is to not say something clearly.

Active voice, in contrast, has two advantages: clarity and credibility.

Active voice advantage #1: clarity

Sentences written in the active voice are clear. Their construction is straight forward, not ambiguous, and generally easier to understand. They say things like, "I love you," not, "you are loved." With the active voice, you know it's me who loves you. With the passive, you're just guessing who's doing the loving.

Active voice advantage #2: credibility

People who write in active voice sound more credible. And because they SOUND more credible, they ARE more credible—if only in the mind of the reader.

This idea of credibility is so important because your perceived credibility and the buyer's perception of risk are inextricably linked. Proposals exist within the context of a sales transaction, and there is almost always some perception of risk in a sales transaction. You're trying to convince someone to choose your product or service that they will use in some strategic or mission critical function. This in itself is risky. You're also trying to convince them to part with their money. Both of these things contribute to a buyer's perception of risk.

No one will adopt your solution or part with their money if they do not perceive you as credible. The less credibility you have, the greater sense of risk they have, and the less likely you are to make a sale. Conversely, the more credible you are, the less risk they perceive, the more likely you are to make a sale.

Active voice will not, by itself, make you credible or your writing clear. But writing in the active voice will contribute to your efforts to write clearly and establish yourself and your company as being credible.

Reiterate to all kickoff attendees that they should be using active voice as they develop their proposal content.

Decide on your tone

The tone you take should vary depending on a number of criteria. In fact, tone can be described in many different ways using many different adjectives. Here are a few I tend to use most frequently:

- **Educational tone.** This is my general default. I typically fall back on an educational tone, especially when I don't always know all of the people who will be reviewing my proposal. When you take an educational tone, you do a lot more explaining. "We do this, and here's why," "We do that, and here's why," and of course, "Here's what this means to you."

- **Competitive tone.** In cases where someone else is the incumbent or you know the buyer prefers another vendor, consider writing with a more competitive tone. Take more opportunities, where appropriate, to differentiate between your solution and competitive solutions. You never want to sound too aggressive, but you don't want to be passive, either.

- **Conservative tone.** In cases where you are the incumbent and you know you are the preferred vendor, consider writing with a more conservative tone. You must still treat the opportunity like it's a new customer you're trying to win—not taking them for granted—just dial down the competitive language so you don't risk sounding too aggressive and, perhaps, coming off negative to the buyers who already know you.

- **Conciliatory tone.** I was involved in one procurement where the buyer went out to bid because their vendor, my client, totally screwed up. First, my client chose the wrong person to run the program. He was not well suited to that role. And then my client didn't genuinely listen to the customer's concerns when they called to complain. When we wrote the executive introduction for the new RFP, therefore, we took a conciliatory tone. Not only did we take responsibility for our screw up, we tried to refocus them on the previous decades-long relationship where things had gone well.

As I mentioned, there are other 'tones' you can take. Regardless, just make certain that everyone in the meeting agrees to using the same one.

Include a benefit statement most of the time

One of the best ways you can make your proposal sound as though it was written by one person is to ensure each writer uses the same techniques. Specifically, make sure your team finishes most of their answers with some kind of benefit statement.

"The benefit to ACME is…"

"The advantage you receive is…"

"By implementing this approach, you get three things…"

Whatever you do, whatever you decide, just make sure everyone who is involved in drafting content shares a mutual understanding of how to approach the writing effort.

8. What is it going to take for us to win?

OK, all the hard work is done. You've spent lots of time analyzing and reviewing, considering and arguing, and now everyone in your proposal strategy meeting has a thorough and comprehensive understanding of what you're proposing, why you're proposing it, how to articulate it, and more. Following all this, there's only one more question to ask:

What's it going to take to win?

I know, this sounds counterintuitive considering all of the work you've just completed, but it's not. Sometimes, often times, it's not possible to see the big picture until you delve into the details.

Maybe you look at all the work you've done, you smile to yourself and say, "we got this." On the other hand, maybe you admit to yourself, "we don't have a chance unless we cut our price by 22%." And sometimes, you may even utter to yourself, "why are we even responding to this RFP? We aren't going to win, and even if we do, we aren't going to make any money at it."

Any writer will tell you that they can have a great outline, a great plan for their book, but as they work drafting the content, as they dig into the details, they discover things they hadn't realized or appreciated at the beginning of the project. In the same way, the people who attend your kickoff meeting will discover things they hadn't realized before. They'll become enlightened.

So now, after everything else has been said, someone needs to stand up and ask in a soft voice, "what's it going to take to win?" Then stop talking and listen.

- Is anyone uncomfortable? You'll see it in their demeanor. Ask them what they're thinking.
- Is anyone hesitant? You'll see it in their demeanor. Get them talking.
- Are people excited and ready to get writing so they can win this? You'll see that, too. End the meeting so they can begin writing.

Just make sure you don't get angry or frustrated if someone isn't fully onboard. It happens, but if you get angry, you'll just discourage people from contributing in the future. And that's a bad thing.

CHAPTER RECAP

Messaging matters. What are we going to say? How are we going to say it? What are the themes we're going to stress? How are we going to differentiate our solution from competitive alternatives?

You must have an effective message. It has to be customer-focused, and it must be consistent across all of the sections of your proposal.

18. Creating Post-Proposal Sales Presentations

Some RFPs are built around a single step buying process while others have two or more. In a single step process, the buyer selects a vendor after reviewing and scoring the proposals they receive. In some procurements, the buyer adds another step into the process; they review the proposals and then select the two or three businesses who will advance. Typically, these "semifinalists" will be invited to deliver an onsite presentation to decision makers.

This chapter includes a variety of best practices and a few tips related to post-proposal sales presentations.

ENSURING SALES MESSAGING CONTINUITY

One of the most important things any business development group can do to improve their proposal win rate is to maintain message continuity between their pre-RFP selling effort, their proposal, and their post-proposal presentations.

> The proposal you submit should be a continuation of the conversations the salesperson was having with the buyer prior to the RFP, and the presentation you deliver should be an extension of the messages you communicated in the proposal.

Unfortunately, this doesn't always happen.

Too often, the proposal team writes an effective proposal and the seller gets invited onsite to deliver a presentation. Then, inexplicably, the salesperson takes back control and dismisses the proposal development team, "Thanks for the help with the proposal, but I got it from here."

This is a common practice, to be sure, but it's not a best practice. In fact, it doesn't even make sense. If the proposal advanced the sale to the short list, shouldn't the proposal team that wrote it be at least minimally involved in helping prepare the presentation? Common sense and an interest in continuity says they should.

The sales team and the proposal team should not be two separate groups working independently, they should be one integrated, unified team working together towards a common cause. This is not only the best practice, it ensures continuity of the sales message from the pre-RFP selling phase to the post-proposal presentation phase.

BUYERS WANT TO HEAR FROM OPERATIONS STAFF

If you submit a proposal and the buyer selects you to go onsite and present, remember that most buyers do not want a presentation from salespeople. This is a bitter pill to swallow for many in the selling community, especially since it's the salesperson who got the opportunity started and has seen it through to this point.

Regardless, buyers want to meet with and hear from the people who are actually going to be delivering the service they're buying.

- If they're buying payroll services, they want to hear from the account manager or payroll manager they'll be working with when they submit their weekly payroll numbers, or the person they will actually be calling every two weeks if they have issues or questions.
- If they're buying IT security software, they want to hear from someone who is an expert in IT security, who can explain with authority and granularity how your solution is going to solve their problems.
- If they're buying medical staffing services, they want to hear from the recruiter who will actually be filling open positions, and hear firsthand this person's familiarity with the market, the challenges it represents, and how she is going to ultimately deliver the results the buyer wants.

See the point? Salespeople are still responsible for orchestrating the whole thing, for bringing in all of the best expert presenters, for managing the overall message and its delivery. But when actually delivering the presentation, the buyer wants to hear from and meet with the experts in your company who are delivering your service to them.

Choosing your presenters

Putting your operations staff in front of buyers is smart, but just as important is choosing the best person for the job. Some people may be experts in their field, but they aren't necessarily good when they're in front of people. Leave these people back in the office where they can use their operations skills to do operations stuff. It's where they belong.

There are some experts, though, who excel in this outward facing role. They don't just come alive in front of other people, *they own it*. When they start talking about what they do, they exude confidence, they ooze credibility, and they inspire trust.

I was once in a meeting where a construction company was hosting a potential buyer. Various people took the podium to talk about their portion of the project, and it was all very pleasant with casual dialogue. Then a site manager got up, dressed in jeans, a little bit of mud still on his boots from a jobsite he just came from—*street creds*. From the moment he opened his mouth, he owned the room. Totally owned it. He oozed credibility. When one of the potential customers said something like, "We had hoped to do it this way," he began shaking his head and said "no you don't and here's why." The entire room was fully engaged, listening intently to every word he spoke. It was amazing.

You need to find *that guy*. He's the one you want presenting when you're down to the 11th hour and everything is on the line. He's the guy that will close the deal and surge you across the finish line.

HOW TO STRUCTURE YOUR PRESENTATION

In some cases, a buyer's invitation to present will be very structured and prescriptive. They may dictate the topics you need to address, the handouts you must provide with each topic, and even the time you can allot to each topic. In these instances, it's important to provide them exactly what they're asking for.

Despite how prescriptive they may be, though, do not forget to make your presentation about them. Give them the information they want, the way they want it, but always include those all-important benefit statements:

- *What this means to you is…*
- *The advantage to you is…*
- *This approach has many benefits, but the most important is…*
- *One of the things you said is important to you is X. With this approach, X is exactly what you get.*

Most other sellers are going to follow the buyer's instructions, and in the process, they're all going to sound the same, like a bunch of feature preachers. Against this cacophony of sameness, you are going to stand out because you've gone the extra step to make it about them.

Solution-focused presentation

Some buyers invite you to present, but they don't provide instructions. So instead of a fill in the blank kind of question, it's more like a great big essay question; you get to choose what you're going to say. It is exactly these situations where many sellers tend to fall back on their seller-focused presentations, *here's who we are, here's what we do, us we me, us we me.*

When faced with an essay question kind of presentation, the best approach is to build a solution-focused presentation that is built around what they want and how you're going to help them get it.

1. Restate what you understand they are trying to achieve

Begin your presentation by restating your understanding about what they want. Include both a list of the challenges that must be overcome along with the outcomes they want.

> *When we receive an RFP, we don't just sit down and figure out how we're going to answer questions. That's what most companies do. What we do is we sit down as a team to review what we understand you want. We discuss it, we analyze it, and we consider it from all angles. Only*

after that do we ask ourselves, "How can we solve this? What's it going to take to get them what they want?"

So, to start our meeting today, I want to begin by reviewing what you want. Now describe what you understand they want.

OK, have I missed anything? Is there anything else we need to include in this?

However you word it, however you configure it, starting your presentation by focusing on them and what they want is ideal. It ensures they understand that you understand their issues and concerns and, ultimately, the outcomes they expect.

2. Overview of the solution you are proposing

Now you get to talk about yourself and the solution you're proposing. Keep your explanation at a fairly high level; it's never good to get bogged down in details too soon or too deeply. If you review a topic and nobody has questions, keep going. That topic is nothing they care too much about.

What is likely going to happen is you get to a topic they care about, and then they'll stop you to ask questions. This is why it's so good to introduce each topic at a high level and to keep moving through your agenda; it saves time for the things they want to talk about in more depth.

3. Explain how your solution overcomes their challenges and delivers the desired outcomes

This part of your presentation may happen and probably should happen at the same time you are presenting your solution. I break it out separately because I want to highlight how important this step is to the overall success of your program.

You began your presentation by reviewing what they want to accomplish, then you described your solution. Now, you have to make certain that you link the two things together. Your solution means nothing to them if it doesn't help them get some outcome they want.

4. Explain how your solution is both different and better than competitive alternatives

In chapter 6, we explored the importance of differentiating your solution from competitive alternatives. I emphasized how difficult it can be, from a buyer's perspective, to understand the differences from one vendor to the next. That argument applies to your presentations just as much as it does to your proposals. In some respects, it's more important. The buyer is actively evaluating, in person, each vendor. The buyer is actively considering the strengths and weaknesses of each. Make your case.

By making your case about why your solution is a better alternative, you're appealing to their reason at that critical point when they are most open to it.

> We understand you have more than a few qualified vendors to choose from. But we also understand there are differences between vendors. These differences are important because they can have a big impact on the outcomes you receive.
>
> Here are three reasons why the solution we are proposing will produce better outcomes for you than any other solution from any other vendor you may be considering...

If you make a compelling statement like this, if you have the courage to say exactly how your solution is different and better than what anyone else is offering, you will make an impact. You may not win, but you'll definitely make an impact.

PRESENTATION TIPS

In addition to everything else we've discussed in this chapter, following are a random smattering of tips and tricks I've collected over the years.

Gather intelligence beforehand

Before an RFP is published, sellers have free rein to call on buyers, to meet with them, get to know them, learn about their issues and interests, etc. After the RFP is published, though, sellers are severely restricted.

Most RFPs include instructions that say something along the lines of, "You cannot speak with anyone in our organization about this RFP, *or else…*" The restriction usually comes with serious warnings and admonitions that sound ominous if not draconian, "If you break this rule, you will be removed from consideration, disallowed, admonished, penalized, and otherwise punished in the severest manner we are legally permitted to pursue." These harsh warning are usually sufficient to discourage most sellers from reaching out to decision makers during the RFP process.

In my experience, though—*and there is admittedly some gray area here*—many buyers don't always enforce the "no contact" restriction into the post-proposal presentation stage of the process. In my experience, it's often permissible, or at least tolerated, for a seller to ask questions about a procurement before they go onsite to present.

> *Hi Tom. I can't tell you how happy we are that you invited us to present to your team. We've started preparing our presentation, and I have a few questions.*

In all the years I've been involved in sales and later in the proposal profession, I've only rarely had anyone push back against this reasonable request. That doesn't mean someone won't, and a few have, but most recognize working with you will provide a better and more focused presentation when you go onsite.

They can always say no.

Be prepared to abandon your presentation

I've always believed the best presentations are those where the buyer completely takes over by asking questions. In my mind, this means they're engaged and they're interested. There are things they want to know as they evaluate your solution.

When this happens, don't be stubborn. Don't stick to your script. Sit back, relax, and let them drive. The better you respond to what they care about, the more likely you're going to win the sale.

Make sure to finish presenting before your allotted time is complete

This is one of those statements that is so obvious, it doesn't need to be said out loud. Except it does.

Always, always, always make sure you are done speaking before your time is up. If they want to keep asking questions, stand there and keep answering. Remember, they can go past your allotted time, that's their right. Just make sure you don't.

CHAPTER RECAP

Post-proposal presentations represent one of your best opportunities to close the deal, but only if you do it well.

Always remember to make it about them, even when you're talking about yourself. Recruit operations staff to deliver the major portions of your presentation. And when you have the freedom, make sure you structure your presentation so it is solution oriented, and so it differentiates your solution from competing alternatives.

19. Responding to RFPs Received Out of the Blue

If you've been reading sequentially, you already know the best practice is to build a proactive selling process, one in which you "make the sale" long before the RFP is issued. Despite this, despite all of your careful planning and proactive efforts, you are inevitably going to receive an RFP out of the blue that you aren't expecting and aren't prepared for. What do you do?

Understanding your chances

Before you take out a pencil and start composing your response, remember that your chances of winning an out of the blue proposal are low. Single digits low. It's difficult to get exact figures because most private organizations do not publish or share their win rate statistics or the practices on which those statistics are based. Still, based on my experience and the experiences of other proposal professionals I know, the average win rate for "out of the blue" proposals is almost always in the single digits.

Accepting your chances of winning are in the low single digits, take a moment and answer these two questions:

- Is it worth the investment in time and money to pursue this RFP since you're likely going to lose?
- Is it worth the opportunity cost—the time this opportunity takes away from other more viable opportunities—to pursue this RFP since you're likely going to lose?

These are decisions only you can make, but if you're serious about winning more business, *at least take the time to ask and answer the questions* before you respond.

Apply some discipline to your decision process

As you work to answer these two questions, and to decide whether you want to respond to the RFP or take a pass, make an effort to apply at least some structure to your process before you put pencil to paper. This process involves addressing these two topics:

1. Evaluate your situation
2. Consider your options

Like most things in life, a little bit of planning and forethought goes a long way, even with RFPs received out of the blue.

EVALUATE YOUR SITUATION

To better evaluate your situation, take some time and answer these five questions.

1. Have you had any substantive conversations with the buyer about this opportunity before the RFP?

If you have not had any substantive conversations with a decision maker about this program, then all you know is what they say in the RFP—and that's not very much. You do not know about the competition, what the buyer thinks of the competition, if any of the decision makers already have vendor preferences or have made vendor decisions, what their pain points are, etc. You are going in blind.

Maybe you were expecting the RFP but just not today. You've had previous substantive conversations, preferably onsite meetings, with one or more decision makers about this program. Based on these conversations, you know something about the decision maker's personal interests and objectives, background about their program, etc. This improves your odds. Still, remember that, despite these conversations, you still didn't know the RFP was coming out today. This suggests there's something going on in the background you don't know about.

One more thing. When I use the term "substantive conversations," I'm talking about conversations with decision makers. Procurement people and contracting staff don't count because, generally, they aren't decision makers. They may be involved in the process, even leading the process, but they don't generally make the purchase decision.

Decisions are usually left up to operations or program staff, or to staff drafted onto a proposal review committee. A contracting officer telling you your product is "exactly what they're looking for" is not a substantive conversation.

2. How much do you know about the account and the opportunity?

This flows from the last question. If all you know is what's written in their RFP, you don't know much. To the point, if you don't know all of the backstory behind what they're asking for in the RFP, you can't possibly tailor your proposal to their specific needs.

For example, suppose they ask a question in their RFP about customer service response times. Knowing nothing more than what is written in the RFP, you might draft a fairly informational answer that is accurate but not necessarily compelling. If you knew the backstory, though, if you knew the buyer's current vendor is woefully inept at responding to calls for assistance, you could build a more persuasive and compelling answer that uses mini-case studies, quotes, documented response times with service levels, etc.

If you don't know the backstory, you don't know much.

3. Do you have history with the buyer? How well do they know you?

One of my clients was working with the Eastern division of a large organization when we got an RFP from the Western division for the same service. No one had ever talked with anyone in the Western division, so this RFP really was 'out of the blue.' We did have the good sense, though, to call some of our contacts in the Eastern division to see if we could learn more. In this case, the program manager in the Western division called the program manager in the Eastern division, and asked him all about our service. We got a good recommendation from our contact.

The point here is even though we didn't talk to the Western program manager, they still learned about us from someone within their own company. I wish we would have known more, but based on these circumstances, pursuing this RFP seemed like an acceptable risk.

4. Is the product or service they want to procure well-aligned with the service you provide?

Do you already sell what they want or will you have to build something to provide the service they require?

Generally, buyers don't want to be your test pilot, a hapless victim of your learning curve. They generally prefer to buy a product that has already been implemented and is in production somewhere else.

If you do not have the product they want, in production, this is a red flag. Think carefully before proceeding.

5. Is this a new procurement or is there an incumbent vendor?

It's tough to unseat an incumbent vendor. That's not to say it doesn't happen, but it's not easy. Generally, unseating an incumbent requires a major sales effort prior to the RFP, and a buyer who is convinced that switching to a new vendor offers more benefits than the risk it introduces. This only happens when they see you as credible, and that only happens when you invest time getting to know them.

If it's a new procurement, your odds are better. It's easier to win a new procurement than it is to unseat an incumbent vendor. Still, they've probably been talking to another vendor, or to other peers who work with another vendor, so that vendor has the upper hand.

By spending time to evaluate your situation, to consider what you know and what you don't, to ponder what you're up against, you'll be in a better position to make an informed decision.

CONSIDER YOUR OPTIONS

Before deciding to respond or walk away, it might be worthwhile to take some time and consider all of your options.

Option #1: Reach out to the contact

RFPs almost always include admonitions that you cannot speak with anyone in the buyer's organization during the course of the procurement. They usually give you a contact person, typically a procurement staff member or a contracting officer, if you have questions.

It's important to understand this contact may know something about the program going out to bid, but not always, and generally not very much. Further, like I mentioned previously, the procurement person generally is not involved in making a purchase decision. Despite all that, with little else to hang your hat on, the procurement person can be a source of information...*but only if approached carefully.*

How to ask procurement officers for information

First, recognize that procurement people are interested and motivated to make certain every procurement is a competitive procurement. When asking for information, therefore, the trick is to tie your request to their motivation. If you call and say, "I'd like to ask some questions about the program," they'll reply with their standard response: "Put it in writing." Then they'll answer your questions, if they choose to, and share those answer with all bidders. Clearly, this doesn't help us.

However, if you turn it around and articulate it like I've done in the following passage, you're framing the conversation; you're making them the salesperson trying to convince you to participate:

> Hi Paul, we received your RFP. Thank you for including us.
>
> We're trying to decide whether or not we should respond. See, we've never talked with anyone at your organization before, and we don't know anything about the program. I'd like to ask a few general questions to get some background.

It's that first statement that's so important: *"We're trying to decide whether or not we should respond."* Now he's thinking to himself that he needs to engage you and convince you to respond. Remember, one of his goals is to make this a competitive procurement.

This approach doesn't always work. Some procurement staff will shut you down like you're a kid asking for dessert before dinner, "no that's against the rules and it's unfair to the other bidders." Still others will reply, with some hesitation, "sure, I can answer a few questions."

If you get this far, be prepared with some basic, non-threatening questions, just enough to get the conversation started.

1. I take it from reading the RFP this is an ongoing program, so I assume you put it out to bid every few years, is that correct?

2. So the last time this program was put out for bid, it was about three years ago?

3. Who is the current vendor?

4. How long have you been working with them?

I'm not asking any super deep questions, or anything that should make him uncomfortable, just some high level background. Further, if I get through just these four questions, I've already learned a lot.

First, I've learned if this procurement is going out on schedule, or if it's going out ahead of schedule. On schedule tells me they're issuing the bid because they have to, not necessarily because they want to. If it's going out ahead of schedule, if it's only been two years since the last RFP, for example, I know something's going on that's causing them to bid early. Nobody bids early unless there's a compelling reason why. So I might even ask a follow up question to clarify, "Why are you going out to bid early?" If it's going out behind schedule, it's been five years instead of three years, they're probably happy with their current vendor, and have issued a couple extensions to the current contract.

Second, I learned who the current vendor is. If I'm in tune with my market, if I've been paying attention to my win/loss record, I know who we compete well against and who we compete poorly against. Either way, it's good information.

Third, I learned how long they've been with their current vendor. If they've been with that vendor for a long time, it's going to be a lot harder to replace them.

Obviously, what you may learn from this effort hardly constitutes a comprehensive dossier, but at least I've learned a few things that will help me decide whether to pursue it.

What if the procurement person is cooperative

One more thing. If your call is going well and the person is being cooperative, get as much as you can and then consider asking to speak with the program manager. Explain your request by saying, "the more I know about the program manager's interests, the better I'll be able to target exactly what it is she wants when we configure our proposal." Most of the time, you get denied and the call stops there. There are those occasions, though, where a forward-looking company will accommodate your request and setup a phone meeting. Not often, but it has happened.

To be clear, this is more likely to happen when the buyer is a business, but almost never when the buyer is a state or local government organization. The difference is businesses are guided by internally-created procurement rules while state and local government procurements are guided by laws and regulations. Some businesspeople are willing to push the rules if they're interested in what you're selling, but most government people would never consider risking it.

Option #2: Consider partnering with another vendor who is in a better position

In some cases, you may consider partnering with a competing organization to provide some component of the solution they propose. For example, suppose the buyer wants a service organization with support offices in six major cities. You already have support offices in two of those cities out West, and one of your competitors has support offices in four of those cities out East. Separately, neither of you meet the minimum program requirements. Together, though, you could provide a more comprehensive solution than either of you could propose separately.

When two organizations build this kind of alliance, one is usually the prime contractor and the other is a subcontractor. You have to decide which is best suited to be the prime, and you also have to decide whether you can work with the other business.

While this approach is not used as often in the B2B world, it's very common in federal government contracting. In fact, it's one of the best ways that businesses new to the federal sector—who otherwise would never be considered for a federal contract—begin developing experience, a reputation, a list of references, and industry relationships.

Option #3: Decline to pursue but leave the door open

If you receive an RFP out of the blue, and you have no relationships or history with the buyer, no inside contacts to guide you, and it represents little more than a shot in the dark, you may consider declining to respond. This is a perfectly acceptable thing to do, and in fact, is often the wisest thing to do.

If you decide to decline, though, make sure you notify the contact who issued the RFP. First, send an email or a letter notifying her that you won't be able to respond at this time, but request that they keep you on their bid list. Make it clear that you'd like to bid the next time they publish the RFP for this program. This ensures you keep your future options open.

Second, follow up with a phone call to verbally thank her for including your company in the bidders list. You may also offer some kind of explanation why you aren't responding.

> *We are in the process of implementing two new clients, and our best resources are stretched thin. We would like to work with you in the future, though, and we would love to be on your bidders list the next time this program goes out to bid.*

Depending on how the call is going, you might also see if you can learn more about their program. For example, if you don't know it, find out who their current vendor is. Even better, see if you can get the name of their internal program manager. The buyer might be protective of that information because she doesn't want you calling on (and bothering) that person while he is in the middle of a procurement today. Still, if you can get it, this could save months of work for your sales staff as they work to find the correct contacts later.

Option #4: Pursue it

If you've been reading sequentially, you know I advise against responding to RFPs received 'out of the blue' because your chances of winning are so low. However, there are still some good reasons to pursue an RFP even if you have little or no chance of winning it.

It's one of your targeted accounts

The RFP is from an organization you included on your targeted account list, even though you haven't begun calling on them yet. So while you probably won't win this particular procurement, responding with a proposal might be a great way to start the conversation. In cases like this, I recommend making your proposal very educational, with an unusually large number of case studies and quotes from your other happy customers.

In a very real sense, treat it almost like a marketing document than a proposal; use it as a tool to launch a conversation after this procurement is completed.

It's a division of a company you already work with

If you already work with one division of a company, and you received an 'out of the blue' RFP from another division, I almost always respond to those unless we are clearly unqualified. Many times, you later learn that while you haven't been talking with the buyer, they've been talking amongst themselves.

Political reasons

A higher up in your company instructs you to respond, even though everyone on your team knows you're going to lose. I hate it when this happens because it's such an irresponsible waste of organizational resources, but it happens all the time.

Shake your head, grumble under your voice, and start writing. This is one instance where your proposal truly is a writing project to complete and NOT a sales opportunity to win. Grumble, grumble.

SCHEDULE A 'STREAMLINED' KICKOFF MEETING

Assuming you decide to respond to the RFP, the next step is to schedule a kickoff meeting so you can plan your proposal development effort.

When you receive an RFP out of the blue, you are at a disadvantage; you are not privy to all of the background knowledge that comes from 12 or 24 months of buyer interaction. All you have is the RFP that's in front of you.

Therefore, while you still need a kickoff meeting to organize your proposal development effort, you also need to streamline the process so it's rightsized for the relatively limited amount of information you have.

Two parts to a streamlined kickoff meeting

Just like your regular kickoff meeting, your streamlined kickoff meeting still has two parts, administrative and sales strategy.

Administrative focus

Administratively, you still need to perform all of the scheduling and logistical items necessary to make certain you complete and submit the proposal on time. This means creating and publishing a proposal development schedule, assigning RFP sections or individual questions to various people within the organization, etc.

Sales strategy focus

From a sales strategy perspective, you must still make an effort to develop a sales strategy so you can both create a message you want to communicate to the buyer and so everyone involved in drafting content understands it.

This involves addressing these four items.

1. Analyze the circumstances surrounding the opportunity

What do you know about the circumstances surrounding the RFP? Are they going out to bid because they have to? Most procurement departments require recurring contracts to be re-bid on a regular basis, like every three, four, or five years. If they're going out to bid because they have to, not because they want to, your prospects of winning are probably low.

If they're going out to bid because they want to, you need to understand why. Here are the most popular reasons why a vendor wants to go out to bid:

- To squeeze the current vendor for a better deal
- The current vendor is falling short
- Economic conditions have changed
- Significant change to program requirements
- Management change

You don't always know why they go out to bid, but if you do, that will help you to understand their motivations, and in turn, how to structure your proposal so it is more focused on them.

2. Analyze the opportunity

Collect as much information as you can from as many sources as you can. Start with the RFP, of course. Analyze it. Scour it. Compare what they say they want to the point scoring system they list.

If you have a database of past RFPs, search for the last RFP they issued and compare that one to this one. This is a great way to see what has changed from the previous procurement to this one.

Look for secondary sources of information about their company. This includes reading their website, and any other properties they may have on social media sites such as Facebook and LinkedIn. Learn as much as you can.

Now that you've collected everything you can, sit around a big conference room table with your proposal development team and then ask and answer these questions:

1. What is their primary issue/ problem/ objective?
2. What are their secondary issues and requirements?
3. Does the current vendor offer some value-added service the buyer would lose if they changed vendors?

These can be difficult to answer if you haven't been actively interacting with the buyer leading up to the RFP release, but do the best you can. Based on your past experience working with other customers, and what you read in their RFP, you can probably come up with some reasonably good though still somewhat generic answers.

3. Configure your solution

You can't write about the solution you are proposing until you actually figure out what you are proposing. This is counterintuitive but, in fact, many organizations start describing their solution without first identifying exactly what their solution is.

Configure and summarize the solution

This is where your business development team creates and drafts the solution you want to propose. Your solution should mention all of the relevant components the customer will want to know about.

List, by line item, the different parts of the solution you are proposing. This may include not just the office copier you are proposing, but also the people you're assigning to the project, the office locations that will be catering to their needs, 24x7 mobile phone access to the president if they ever have a problem they can't resolve, etc.

Write it down and share it with the entire team.

Include non-traditional components that add value

When we think like sellers, we often think in terms of what we're selling. When we think like buyer's, though, we tend to view what we're buying in a more comprehensive, holistic way—not just what we're buying but the totality of what we get.

I once talked with a buyer, a client of one of my clients, who shared that while she valued the service we provided, she valued even more the access she had to our SMEs who were so knowledgeable about the field.

If she had a question, she could call one of our staff and get a mini-education that, time after time, allowed her to make informed decisions.

View the project from the buyer's perspective and you'll configure a solution that more effectively gives them everything they want.

4. Configure your message

So far, you've taken time to understand the circumstances surrounding the bid, discussed the buyer and their needs, and configured the solution you want to propose. As you transition into this next phase of the meeting, your goal is to discuss messaging and decide how you want to communicate your solution to the buyer.

To be clear, the solution you created in the last step is different from the messaging you use to communicate it. The solution solves their problem but the messaging is how you explain it to them. This is where you tell them how your solution is going to get them what they want.

When you walk out of this meeting, there must be a shared understanding among all business development team members about what your message is and how you are going to express it to the buyer. To that end, you should ask a series of questions.

- How is the solution you are proposing going to address the buyer's primary issue?
- Focus on the secondary requirements: how are you going to address/solve the top five?
- What advantages do you have, within the context of this particular opportunity, compared to the competition?
- What are your competitors' advantages compared to yours? How are you going to overcome them?
- What shortcomings do you have to overcome? Where do you fall short of their requirements? How are you going to overcome them?
- What is your style and tone?
- What is it going to take for you to win?

All of these questions, and how you approach them, have been addressed at length in the chapter titled, *Configure your message*. You can read more about each in that chapter.

The important point is this; make certain you take the time to ask the questions and, as a team, work through how you want to answer them. The talking points you produce become the message you share.

CHAPTER RECAP

When you get an RFP out of the blue, your chances of winning are low. If you put some discipline to your decision process, though, you'll be using better reasoning that will necessarily result in better decisions.

- **Evaluate your situation**. Figure out if you even have a chance.
- **Consider your options**. You don't have many options, but you do have some. Consider each of them.
- **Schedule a 'streamlined' kickoff meeting**. If you decide to pursue it, schedule a streamlined kickoff meeting to make certain you have a good solution, a good message, and everyone who is writing content is on the same page.

Reference and Index

Glossary

Some of the definitions listed here were referenced in this book. Others are terms that, while not specifically used in this book, you might hear when working with or around proposal and business development people.

11th hour decision maker

The 11th hour decision maker is a derogatory term for a senior manager who can never find time to participate in proposal strategy meetings when a proposal is being developed. Instead, this short-sighted manager waits until the proposal team has a response almost completed, and then he swoops in at the 11th hour to see what's being proposed and to make changes—often big, complicated changes that fundamentally alter the solution and dramatically impact content throughout the proposal.

Don't be an 11th hour decision maker. You're not helping anyone, you're making things worse not better, and nobody likes you.

AEC industry

AEC is an abbreviation for architecture, engineering, and construction. This industry relies heavily on RFPs and proposals to transact business.

Association of Proposal Management Professionals (APMP)

The Association of Proposal Management Professionals, APMP, is a professional organization dedicated to the business of proposals. According to their website, the organization "promotes the professional growth of its members by advancing the arts, sciences, and technologies of winning business."

APMP is an international organization with chapters in many countries and regions. You can learn more about the organization at their website, APMP.org.

Chunking

Chunking is proposal industry jargon sometimes used by proposal professionals. It refers to editing a large, uninterrupted section of text into smaller chunks, each of which is preceded by a bold heading. For a typical business person who favors skimming your proposal rather than reading it, chunking dramatically improves readability.

Color teams

Federal government contractors typically rely on "color teams" to perform various reviews at various stages of the proposal development process. A blue team, for example, is focused on reviewing the proposal's outline structure. The pink team, in contrast, is focused on the content that's been added to the outline. Then there's the red team, the green team, the gold team, the white team, and any other sub-process team colors you care to invent. Chartreuse? Vermillion? Puce?

Color team reviews make sense for many larger organizations that run sophisticated business and proposal development operations. In these environments, color team reviews are a best practice.

I've never fully embraced this color-coded system. It's partly because I'm colorblind; I always seem to show up at the wrong meeting. Aside from that, this multi-team approach is too involved for most small and midsize businesses to implement. Most lack the resources for something so sophisticated.

Whatever review process you decide to use, regardless of whether it uses colors, make sure it is both right-sized and fully "implementable" for your business.

Column fodder

When buying organizations launch a procurement, they often know from the outset the one or two vendors they are most likely going to select. Still, contracting staff want the procurement to at least appear competitive because corporate rules or government regulations require it. Therefore, they reach out to competing sellers and invite them to bid. They might even tell you your product "looks like a perfect fit" for what they're buying. Don't be gullible. Don't buy into this argument.

The truth is you probably don't have a chance at winning because they've already picked someone else or narrowed the field down to a few that don't include you. In fact, the only reason they talk to you nicely and act as though you have a chance at winning is because, more than anything, they want you to write a proposal in response to their RFP. If you do, you're providing them a valuable service; you're filling up another column in their vendor spreadsheet so they can report to their managers that the procurement is competitive. This is the definition of column fodder.

When this happens to you, you've officially been column foddered. I know, it sounds dirty. It feels dirty, too. But when you realize that most business development people have also been column foddered before, some repeatedly, you start feeling better about yourself.

Formal procurement

A formal procurement is a method organizations use for procuring goods and services that are either expensive or strategically important. In most cases, an organization will convene a group or committee responsible to document requirements or specifications for the product or service being acquired, draft a solicitation (typically a request for proposal), and then review the vendor proposals that are submitted in response.

Formal procurements take all the fun out of buying stuff, but major organizations maintain they result in better purchase decisions.

Ghosting (the competition)

"Ghosting the competition" is proposal industry jargon. Ghosting is a competitive tactic to take advantage of a competitor's weakness. For example, if you are pursuing a contract and you know your biggest competitor is in chapter 11 bankruptcy reorganization, you might ghost them by saying something like this: "Unlike some vendors in this market who are struggling with debt and financial issues as they try to reorganize, our company continues to be financially strong, consistently profitable, and debt free."

You have to be careful when ghosting the competition; you don't want to sound arrogant, boastful, or mean. Still, most buyers want to know where you're better and, especially, if another vendor is weak or struggling.

Gross win ratio

The gross win ratio offers an easy way to measure the overall effectiveness of your proposal efforts. While it's too general to offer in-depth understanding, it's a simple and easy way to measure overall progress going forward.

The gross win ratio is calculated by dividing the total number of RFP opportunities you've won by the total number of RFPs to which you've responded. For example, if you responded to 100 RFPs and you won 60, then you divide 60 by 100 to come up with a win ratio of .6, or 60%.

IDIQ (indefinite delivery, indefinite quantity)

IDIQ stands for *indefinite delivery, indefinite quantity*. It is a kind of contract that organizations use when they want to buy goods or services, they don't know exactly how much they will be buying, but they still want to get a negotiated rate. For example, suppose an organization buys office copier paper for 50 offices over a five state region. They could have someone run down to the corner office supply store each time they needed more paper, but they'd be paying full retail each time. As an alternative, they may negotiate an IDIQ contract at a better-than-retail price. Even though they don't know exactly how much paper they'll need, they know they'll need a good amount, so why not get a better price?

Informal procurement

An informal procurement is a buying process that organizations use when the procurement does not exceed a particular price or the product being acquired is not strategically important. Depending on the organization, it may still require that certain procurement rules be followed, or that the buyer seeks bids from more than one company, but it's nowhere near as complex or structured as a formal procurement involving an RFP.

Kickoff meeting

A well-designed kickoff meeting has two fundamental components; an administrative function and a sales strategy function.

The administrative portion of the meeting includes everything typically included in a traditional proposal kickoff meeting: creating and publishing a proposal development schedule and firm deadlines, assigning RFP sections or individual questions to various writers, deciding what research must still be done and assigning those tasks to staff members, etc.

The sales strategy function is itself twofold; it involves figuring out what it's going to take to win, and then making sure all team members share that understanding. The sales strategy portion of the meeting should dominate the majority of the time you allot to your meeting and planning effort. That's because while assigning administrative tasks is *important*, a targeted, customer-focused sales strategy is *critical*. Indeed, the project's success or failure hinges on how well you complete this step.

Presentation win ratio

Many procurements are organized into multiple steps. For example, the buyer may evaluate the proposals that are submitted by each vendor, and then they choose two or three vendors they want to investigate further. These sellers are typically invited onsite to deliver a presentation to the people who will be making the ultimate buying decision. This is often called "making it to the short list" or being "shortlisted."

The presentation win ratio measures the effectiveness of your onsite presentations. If you are invited to present 10 times, and you win a contract or advance to the next step five times, then your presentation win ratio is 50%.

Prime contractor

To compete effectively, a vendor may sometimes partner with another vendor so, together, they offer a solution that meets the minimum qualifications. In these cases, one vendor will be the prime contractor and other vendors will be subcontractors. The prime contractor is the organization that signs the contract with the seller and is ultimately responsible for delivering the product or service.

Probability of winning (PWin)

Probability of winning, or PWin, is a calculation designed to give sellers insight into their chances of winning a particular procurement. PWin can be calculated many different ways, from manual and entirely subjective reviews to highly sophisticated programs that calculate PWin based on key performance indicators (KPIs).

Most small to medium-sized businesses don't have the resources to invest in sophisticated PWin systems to guide their decisions. Besides, in many organizations, the decision to proceed is often based more on political considerations or force of someone's personality than on objective data.

Still, if the managers can at least do a basic review of an opportunity before anyone begins writing, they may save themselves lots of time by walking away from opportunities they likely won't win.

Protest

A protest is a formal objection submitted by a seller to a government buyer when the seller believes a procurement has been awarded incorrectly because it violates law or regulations, didn't follow the rules, or is in some way unfair. There are different justifications for submitting protests, so you have to understand the applicable laws and regulations before submitting the protest. This is why sellers will often work with attorneys to prepare their protests.

Too often, protests are being submitted these days not because the buyer did something wrong but because the seller is a sore loser and doesn't like that their competitor won instead of them. These protests almost never win, they might give the protester a bad name, and they muddy the water for the rest of us when we actually have a legitimate protest.

Qualifying (an opportunity)

A salesperson can easily waste a significant amount of time and resources pursing a sales opportunity that is "not a good fit" for the product or service she's selling. Therefore, all professional salespeople are taught to "qualify" sales opportunities.

Qualifying a sale means the salesperson and sales manager go through a process whereby they evaluate the merits of the new opportunity against some objective criteria they've already established. For example, a seller might determine, for an opportunity to be well-qualified, it must meet the following criteria:

- It must involve a financial commitment above $500,000.
- The primary contact person must be director level or above with budget authority.
- The buyer must be interested in blue copiers rather than red.
- The opportunity is ideal if they're currently working with Dave's Fictional Copier Company, but it's still a favorable opportunity if they're currently working with Donna's Fictional Copier Company.

Ironically, many salespeople fail to apply the same qualification discipline when responding to RFPs that they would otherwise apply to any other sales opportunity they encounter. In other words, they get an RFP in the door and, almost by default, choose to respond to the RFP— *even though they know nothing about the opportunity*. This approach is not only undisciplined, it generally wastes lots of resources.

Request for proposal

A request for proposal (RFP) is a formal document, published by a company or government entity, that requests vendors submit structured proposals in response to a list of specifications, requirements, or questions.

RFPs are generally far longer than they need to be, poorly organized, lack clarity, and almost always mandate unreasonable requirements and unreasonable response timeframes. Further, it's not uncommon for some RFPs to be issued immediately prior to a national holiday and mandate response due dates immediately after the same holiday.

It's a little known fact outside the proposal community, but true nevertheless, that Dante created a special place in hell—between the third circle (gluttony) and fourth circle (greed)—for procurement officers who set proposal due dates within a week following a national holiday.

Request for information

A request for information (RFI) is a formal document, published by a company or government entity, that requests vendors submit structured documents in response to a list of questions.

RFIs are often used before RFPs. They are used by buyers to inform themselves about features or capabilities they may want to incorporate into their procurements and, in some cases, to exclude certain vendors who do not meet minimum qualifications.

Request for qualifications

In some industries, the engineering field in particular, a request for qualifications (RFQ) is almost identical to an RFP; it describes a project, lists the specifications, and asks respondents to submit a proposal in response. Despite the difference in naming, it's still a proposal and you still have to be customer-focused and persuasive.

Request for quote

A request for quote (RFQ) is a solicitation where a buyer requests the vendor respond with a quote for a particular product or service.

RFQ

An RFQ can refer to either a 'request for qualifications,' or a 'request for quote.' A request for qualifications is much like an RFP, and is most commonly used in engineering fields. A request for quote is a request for a firm price quote for a specific product or service.

Shortlist

Some procurements use a two-step process. After reviewing all of the proposals submitted, they may choose three vendors who advance to the shortlist. This is commonly referred to in the industry as being shortlisted.

Shortlisted vendors are typically invited onsite to conduct a presentation to decision makers. Presumably, whoever makes the best presentation wins.

Short list win ratio

Many procurements are organized into multiple steps. For example, the buyer may evaluate the proposals that are submitted by each vendor, and then choose two or three they want to investigate further. This is often called, "making it to the short list." The two or three sellers who make it to the short list are typically invited onsite to deliver a presentation to the people who will be making the ultimate buying decision.

The short list win ratio offers insight into the effectiveness of your proposals. It is calculated by dividing the number of times you make it to the short list divided by how many proposals you submit in response to RFPs. For example, if you submit 100 proposals, and you advance to the short list seventy-five times, then you divide seventy-five by 100 to come up with a short list win ratio of 75%.

Skimmability

Skimmability refers to how well a section of text can be quickly skimmed by a busy reviewer who lacks the time or motivation to read the entire proposal document. A good skimmability quotient means your document is easy to skim and will be well-received by most reviewers. A poor skimmability quotient means no one is going to spend any time looking at your proposal. Sorry.

SLED

SLED is an abbreviation for state and local government agencies and educational organizations. SLED organizations typically rely heavily on formal procurements to acquire goods and services.

SME

Abbreviation for "subject matter expert."

Solicited proposal

A solicited proposal is a proposal document written in response to a formal solicitation, and can take the form of a request for proposal (RFP), request for information (RFI), request for quote (RFQ), or request for qualifications (RFQ).

In some cases, it may also refer to a marriage proposal solicited by a shotgun-toting father after learning his daughter is pregnant.

Subcontractor

A vendor may sometimes partner with another vendor so, together, they offer a solution that meets the minimum qualifications of a particular procurement. The prime contractor is the organization that signs the contract with the seller and is ultimately responsible for delivering the product or service. A subcontractor signs a contract with the prime contractor, and provide a subset of the overall product or service.

Subject matter expert

A subject matter expert, commonly abbreviated SME, is a person who has expertise in a particular subject or area. Within the context of proposal development, a person does not necessarily need an advanced degree or certification to be considered an SME. For example, an accounting clerk who has experience integrating the seller's invoicing system with external accounting programs might be considered an SME because he or she has expertise in a particular area.

Despite this generally accepted definition, some members of the proposal community insist the abbreviation actually stands for, "Some May be Experts." This implies some may not be experts, and don't contribute that much to the process, but they pretend to be experts since it offers them higher pay and prestige as if they were actual experts. See *11ᵗʰ hour decision maker*.

Thud Factor

Conceived and made famous by author and proposal consultant Dr. Tom Sant, the Thud Factor is Sant's attempt to explain why so many proposal writers feel compelled to produce such lengthy and weighty proposal documents. Lacking any other logical explanation, Sant asserts that some proposal writers believe buyers make purchase decisions based solely on the weight of the proposals submitted; "they drop all of the proposals on a table and the one that makes the biggest 'thud' wins."

While Sant's logic is unassailable, little research has so far been presented to confirm whether proposal weight, thud volume, or measurable seismic disruptions are actually used in strategic purchase decisions.

Unsolicited proposal

An unsolicited proposal is a proposal sent to a buyer that is not in response to a formal procurement document such as an RFI, RFP, or RFQ. Often, a salesperson is speaking with a buyer, and the buyer says something like, "this is interesting, I want to show it to others, please send me a proposal." Even though they ask for it, it's still generally considered unsolicited in the sense it was not requested in response to a formal solicitation.

An unsolicited proposal can also refer to assertive romantic propositions made to pretty girls by guys who, based on a prodigious consumption of alcohol prior, believe they actually have a shot.

Index

Bibliography

Cialdini, R. (2001). *Influence: science and practice--4th ed.* Needham
    Heights: Allyn & Bacon.

Dickson, C. *One simple thing you can do to greatly improve your proposal
reviews.* Retrieved from https://proplibrary.com/proplibrary/item/238-
one-simple-thing-you-can-do-to-greatly-improve-your-proposal-
reviews/

Heiman, S. (1985). *Strategic Selling: the unique sales system proven
    successful by America's best companies.* New York: William
    Morrow and Company, Inc.

Parkinson, M. (2010). *Do-It-Yourself Billion Dollar Graphics: 3 fast and
    easy steps to turn your text and ideas into persuasive graphics.*
    Annandale: PepperLip Press.

Sant, T. (2012). *Persuasive Business Proposals: writing to win more
    customers, clients & contracts--3rd ed.* New York: AMACOM.

Strunk, W. (1972). *The Elements of Style--2nd ed.* New York: Macmillan.

Weinberg, M. (2013). *New Sales. Simplified.: the essential handbook for
    prospecting and new business development.* New York:
    AMACOM.